MIND BLOW
Understanding Consciousness

Sufi George

SUFI GEORGE BOOKS
Tucson

Copyright ©2009 by George Arthur Lareau. All rights reserved under International and Pan-American Copyright Conventions. No part of this work may be reproduced or transmitted in any form by any means, electronic or mechanical, including photocopying and recording, or by any information storage or retrieval system, except as may be expressly permitted by the 1976 Copyright Act or in writing by the author.

ISBN 978-1-885570-40-6

Sufi George Books: http://sgbooks.sufigeorge.net

Table of Contents

Introduction 5
Introduction to the Nature of Truth 9
Our Minds Create Four Kinds of Truth 13
The Generic Human Being 19
Our Consciousness of Mind and Body 31
My Life Is Such a Mess 35
Figuring Out Your Ego 39
The Human Experience of Reality 41
The Components of Consciousness 57
Attention 61
Where Is Our Attention Focused? 65
Intuition Demystified 69
A Guided Tour of Our Consciousness 73
Figure One 83
The Role of Emotion in Consciousness 87
We Are Living In Two Universes! 91
Soul? 97
Enlightenment Clearly Explained 101
The Stages of Understanding 105
Locate Your Crosshair 107
Get a Peek of Your Alpha Self 109
Consciousness Principles from Science 113
The Categories of Things 128
About Patterns 133
Orbits, the First Pattern 135
The Amazing Life of an Antimaterial Dot 138

Carrier Waves Illustrating the FEAR "Typical Response Pattern"... 157
Do You Feel Vibes from Others? The Rules of Resonance 161
Create Reality with Morphic Robots 165
Some Key Morphic Robots.. 171
Where Does a Habit Get Its Power? 175
Thoughts on Purpose... 177
Who Are You? 179

Introduction

We are very fortunate people. For the first time in our history, we can understand our consciousness.

Presented here is a dynamic model of consciousness that demonstrates each component and how they work together as a system.

Understanding this model of consciousness leads to a completely new perspective on ourselves and our reality. With this perspective, it becomes possible to purposefully manage (recreate) ourselves, our lives, and our reality.

This model is made possible by a number of scientific discoveries about the nature of reality, and by applying those discoveries to the aspects of consciousness that are undeniably apparent from analytical introspection.

The model reveals the human potentials that have been discussed and promised throughout the ages, and makes obvious the techniques for realizing these potentials.

Because this understanding or perspective is dramatically different from our common sense view of ourselves and our reality, it can be difficult to grasp at first.

The key to understanding the model is to forget, or at least set aside, what we think we know, and develop this new perspective from scratch.

The articles in this book are designed to help you achieve this new perspective. Each article has its own slant and purpose.

The model of consciousness is to be visualized. The components are given physical descriptions to aid in visualization. The physical descriptions are accurate, not necessarily as what consciousness actually looks like (although, why not?), but as components that have specific characteristics and interrelationships.

These physical descriptions are to be personally confirmed in several ways, which are given. These confirmations provide the proof of the model's accuracy.

For a long time now, the thing we call consciousness has been shrouded in mystery, religion, superstition, belief, speculation and confusion.

Thanks to certain branches of science, the knowledge of mankind has now progressed to the point where consciousness may be discussed without any need for blind faith or speculative belief.

My goal here is to present a clear, generic understanding of consciousness based on a foundation of scientific discoveries and indisputable personally observable phenomena that are obvious within ourselves, once we look at them.

The significance of scientific fact is that it is arrived at through consensus among experts, through rigid processes that are meticulously designed and used by all in the same way.

When a scientist establishes a scientific fact, it must be verifiable by any other expert in the field, and even a single instance of disproof invalidates it.

Thus, scientific fact is the finest approach to truth that mankind has developed, and, if truth really is our goal, we should be grateful for it and do our best to scoop it up.

I'm no scientist myself. I've relied on the works of those authors who have presented this difficult material in books that can be understood by a layman.

However, the result here is a model of consciousness that is simple and that can be personally verified. The empowerment that comes with understanding it is further verification. It isn't necessary to plow through the scientific literature to grasp this. The model stands on its own.

Introduction to the Nature of Truth

As we discuss the nature of truth, you will be wondering if what I have to say about it agrees with what you think about it.

When we agree, you'll think I'm quite a marvel, and when we disagree, you'll think I'm wrong. This is how we are, but it's too bad because it makes it difficult for us to approach new ideas without prejudice, with an open mind.

The search for truth requires self-honesty. Self-honesty reveals that we have doubts about many things, that we don't really know it all. It reveals where we've sold ourselves a bill of goods because something felt right and not because it was the god's honest truth. It reveals where we've settled for less than a best effort in arriving at what we believe to be true, where we've taken the easy way out.

Many people think truth is made of steel. Even if it were, steel, like everything else, is made of frequency waves. These waves are in motion, so there is constant change in the fundamental aspect of steel. It is not really standing still, and it is not permanent.

At the practical level, this is no problem, and that is the way it is with truth, too. At the practical level, truth can be functional and useful, but it can't be permanent and unchanging.

Dogmatism of any kind is alien to the nature of truth, even when we believe some dogma as the absolute truth. If you've looked at several dogmatic systems, you've noticed that every one of them claims to have the absolute truth, which wouldn't be possible if there were only one absolute truth.

In the past, before mass communications, rapid travel and other changes that have made it a small world, people lived in groups that were often influenced very little by outside groups. In those days, it was possible for a community to share a dogmatic belief system without encountering much adverse influence from other communities. Today, it is a simple matter to learn about other religions and metaphysical systems, so dogmatists frequently encounter conflicting beliefs from outside.

Self-honesty, which dogmatists deliberately avoid, raises the questions: Which one is really the truth? Why would one bother to argue over one's truth? If you know that something is true, why does it bother you that someone else thinks differently? Why is it important to be right in the eyes of others? Isn't it satisfying enough to know that one is right inside? Why do you care about what someone else thinks is true? Why defend your truth? Why reinforce your truth? Is it because we doubt? Because we know, down deep, that maybe our truth isn't so true? That we aren't really sure?

What we call truth is relative truth, relative to the person who has it. Your truth is true for you, but not necessarily for me or anyone else. Our truths are necessarily different, and that's why we're able to argue about them. Each of us can only believe such truth. We can never know that we've arrived at the perfect last word.

We cannot force ourselves to believe anything rigidly and get away with it. To attempt to do so only builds to a day when there is a sudden shock revealing the charade, for growth must find its crack in the sidewalk and will not be stopped. Truth is a growing thing.

In this discussion of truth, there will be some ideas that are probably new to you. Examine them, understand them, and compare them with what you have now. Leave yourself open to the possibility of finding new ideas about truth that are useful for you. I'm not going to make this discussion complicated. In fact, I've developed a model that shows quite clearly how we create our truth, and which shows us a lot about the nature of truth. I call this the "Three Peaks" model.

Our Minds Create Four Kinds of Truth

What is truth? An important question, right?

The only truth that can be called universal or absolute is the truth of our awareness, and this truth does not come from the mind. It doesn't "come from" anywhere. It's an immediate, direct knowing. The truth of awareness is the only truth that is the same everywhere.

Truth from the mind is always less than universal. It is relative truth.

Mind develops truth in four basic ways: blind faith, speculation, reason and science.

Faith

Each person has a personal set of truths created by mind, and like snowflakes, no two sets are identical.

These truths begin to accumulate in childhood when they are taken on blind faith (seeing and hearing are believing). The resulting truths can be satisfying, until the mind develops further.

A blind faith truth can only be accepted and believed. It does not go through any process of discernment or discrimination, and certainly is never rational.

As children, we accept and believe whatever truth is handed to us. We have nothing to compare it with, and no reason to question it.

We believe many things that later turn out to be false. We believe in Santa Claus and the tooth fairy, for example, only to find them false later on.

But many blind faith truths are never challenged and persist into adulthood. Moral and religious truths are in this category. Fact is, we have no more basis for continuing to believe these truths than we do for believing in Santa Claus. Blind faith is blind faith.

Way back in time, when we were hunted animals, we had no time to do anything more than monitor our environment for food and threats to our lives.

We depended entirely on what we saw, heard or otherwise sensed. Our reality consisted only of this. Our acceptance of this reality was a matter of blind faith.

Speculation

As mind developed, speculation began the creative process of considering additional possibilities.

Speculative truth involves imagination. Anything goes. The main difference between blind faith and speculation is that speculation gives us more possibilities of things to believe, things that are in addition to the material world as experienced.

The variety of speculative truths is spectacular. Since there are no rules for creating this kind of truth, the products of speculation can be anything.

When we developed in time to the point where we could enjoy some leisure, some measure of safety that allowed us to shift from physical reality to the reality within, we began to imagine possibilities that were not present in physical reality.

With the development of imagination, mythologies became possible, and we devised lots of them. We used mythologies to explain everything from the creation of the universe to our purposes in being alive.

Today, we are born with both capacities, blind faith and speculation. That is, we don't have to develop these approaches to truth; they are there within us.

Reason

Mind can be trained to follow rational thought process. One advantage of rational thought process is that it is the collective effort and property of a community without boundaries.

Thus, rational truth is not merely personal truth, but truth with consensus. Consensus makes the difference between private experience and shared experience, and promotes broader community.

Rational thought process is a recent development in the human mind, relatively speaking. It began roughly 3500 years ago, with the Greeks.

Today, we are not born with rationality. It must be learned. We have the capacity for learning it, but unless we train our minds in rational thought process, we do not progress beyond blind faith and speculation.

Science

In our century, after just 300 years of development, science has become our most trusted approach to the creation of truth.

Interestingly, it has now arrived at many of the same conclusions as centuries of speculative metaphysics. This is new in the history of mankind.

Science adds the confirmation of experimental proof to the specialization of rational thought process. As practiced by highly trained and able humans, science produces our highest quality consensual truth.

This truth comes from our superior thinkers worldwide. Science is largely responsible for establishing global community as a new paradigm.

The truth of science is not perfect. It's merely superior to any other product of the human mind (defining the mind as a thought processor and not as consciousness itself).

So even at its best, the human mind has not produced absolute truth. Quite the contrary. Science proves to us that any truth created by the mind is relative truth.

Consider the Source

When we find ourselves questioning or defending one of our truths, we can track down which level of our mind it's coming from.

Is it simply an issue of blind faith? Is it our private conclusion based on speculation? Is it reasoned out? Does it come from science?

This ranking of levels of truth shows us the quality of a truth. The highest quality of truth by the mind comes from science.

Now, unless we are scientists ourselves, scientific truth brings us back to faith, faith in science. But this faith can be strengthened by developing our basic understanding of scientific process.

By understanding the rigid processes used by scientists, including the requirement of experimental proof, we can justify our faith in science.

This may never give us absolute truth. While we may desire absolute truth, we've never had it before except by kidding ourselves, so we must face the fact that truth from the mind is relative.

The only absolute truth we do have does not come from the mind. It is the self-evident truth of our awareness.

Even better than this, we can have scientific truth that describes and agrees with our self-evident awareness. When mind and intuition agree, that's as good as truth gets. And it's never happened before in our history, only now in our privileged lifetimes.

The Generic Human Being

Enlightenment is an experience that changes the way we understand who and where we are. Although in the past it has been cloaked in mystery, symbolism, ritual, fantasy, and so on, today enlightenment is within the reach of any serious student. Today, enlightenment can be achieved by following a modern path that satisfies the rational mind and produces the unforgettable enlightenment experience itself.

Understanding who and where we are is the crux of the matter. Our common sense about this is wrong. If we think we are the physical body living in a material world, we are wrong. Many of today's modern physicists know this and are trying to tell us this.

When I was a high school freshman in 1953, our physical sciences teacher explained that the atom was made mostly of space, and like students everywhere we asked why, if that were true, we couldn't push our hands through our desks. But it is true, and laughing it off isn't the right approach to understanding it.

Let's imagine that I'm giving a demonstration at a lecture. I have a yellow ball on a string, and I'm spinning it around. Just then, someone enters the lecture hall, and he sees a yellow loop in front of me. I invite him to come up to the stage.

He says, "I see you have a yellow loop in front of you."

I say, "No, I'm afraid you're mistaken. I have a yellow ball in front of me."

He is skeptical. He gingerly touches the surface of the loop, and quickly pulls his finger back when he feels the loop. He touches the loop carefully in another spot, then another. Finally, he says, "I'm afraid it's a loop because no matter where I touch it, I can feel it. If it were a ball, it would be in only one place and my chances of touching it would be very slim indeed!"

Really, I can't fault his thinking. He believes what he's seeing and feeling, and usually we trust our senses to deliver correct information to us. He has direct evidence to support his conclusion. I don't know how to argue with him, so I decide to simply reveal to him that I actually have a ball on a string. I stop spinning it, and the ball hangs there.

Of course he is forced to change his thinking now, but he does so the same way as before—he believes his senses, what he's seeing. And since his senses have just given him conflicting conclusions, first that it's a loop, then that it's a ball, how can he trust either conclusion?

So, seeing is not believing. What I see when I look at you is a lot of frequency waves, light waves that go into my eyeballs and impact with the retina at the back of the eyeball. From there, they change. They are no longer visible, no longer light. They change frequency and stimulate chemical and electrical signals. When these signals finally reach the place in our minds where we assemble them into something meaningful, we can "see" them. But we are seeing them inside, in blackness. We are seeing a mental model.

The light waves I see are not reflected by empty space; they're reflected by those tiny particles that make up atoms. If I touch your hand, I'm feeling the ball on a string, the rapid passing of subatomic particles.

You are realizing, I'm sure, that time is the glue that holds our material reality together. If time were stopped, the ball on a string would be suspended in one spot. We'd be living in a still photograph. Certainly boring.

Time is different in an atom. Particles are orbiting at speeds of millions of cycles per second. When a ball on a string travels that fast, the loop can seem to be as solid as steel.

Such a speed is impossible for us to perceive directly. Consider that motion pictures are projected at 24 frames (or cycles) per second. When we're able to see the ball 24 times in a second, it appears to be a loop, or a continuous reality. This is so slow compared to the speeds in an atom that we have no hope of seeing the particles in an atom with our eyes, even if they were large enough to see directly. We can only see the loops, the illusions.

But our physicists can see them, using proper equipment. They know they're there. They know that reality is made of this. And we need to learn this from them. Once this concept sinks in, our perspective on reality will change.

Before science, we had belief and superstition. While these

are still very active today, as religions, mystery schools, etc., they are in fact outmoded now. Today, we have scientific explanations for all of the essential metaphysical questions, and we can give up mere belief and superstition.

I've studied numerous metaphysical schools and traditions, practiced meditation and other disciplines for decades, and read over 5,000 books in my search for understanding the nature of myself and reality. I was looking for what the various schools and traditions had in common, assuming that they were all discussing enlightenment as a natural phenomenon.

The only common thread I found was that they all referred to what we today call alternate reality. That is, they were all based on experience of a reality other than our everyday material world. In some cases these were visions, in others they were dreams.

The worldwide variety of such experiences is overwhelming and confusing; but today, such experiences are well understood by lucid dreaming, a new science (psychophysiology). Lucid dreaming has proven that there really is an alternate reality, and that it can be just as real, or even "more real," than our material reality.

Lucid dreams are dreams in which the dreamer becomes aware that he is dreaming. In such a dream, the dreamer can learn to control, even create, his dreams. In fact, in such a dream, anything that can be imagined is possible. The experience of lucid dreaming is vivid, vibrant, and very real.

When we are confronted with two very different kinds of reality, material and lucid dreaming, what are we to conclude about the nature of reality?

First of all, reality is what we experience; it's the sense we make of incoming frequency wave signals, or the meaning we find in them. Secondly, reality is not "out there" as much as it is inside ourselves; what's out there is frequency waves bouncing off particles, and our reality is a personal mental model, a personal interpretation of signals. Thirdly, our experience of reality is not true; our senses deceive us, and our minds don't understand it.

We need to change our truth before we can accept all of this. It may be that truth is something we've always taken for granted, but that's no longer enough. We need to realize the relative nature of truth, an understanding that Einstein gave us a century ago.

I've developed a model of how we create our truth. With this model, we can see that truth is relative to the information that we get and how we interpret it, and that it varies with the individual. The simplest illustration of the uniqueness of truth to the individual is the fact that in space it is not possible for two people to share the same spot, so they see different things.

The model, from my book *Three Peaks, A Model for Understanding Truth,* describes the sources from which we get our data, how they interact within us, what they produce, and what we can conclude. I summarize the model in this book.

No two people can be expected to have the same truths, because their root sources are different and their observations are different. People who join belief-based organizations must admit that conformity to such beliefs requires some force-fitting.

It is misguided to attempt to make people believe the same thing. One wouldn't want to make them all look alike, so why make them all think alike? It is unnatural and just not the way things overwhelmingly are.

With an understanding of the relative nature of truth, one may still quest for some truth beyond that. After all, relative truth resides in the rational mind, and that's local. However, it is important to satisfy the rational mind when it continually nags and pesters you about what you're doing or the direction you're going in or the details you're deliberately overlooking. It must be satisfied that it has finished its job of producing high quality truth, and then it will let you go on to the next step.

Using one's understanding of the relative nature of truth, one can then critically examine modern scientific truth without holding emotional suspicions about it, and appreciate the marvel that it is.

The common themes in a personal quest for enlightenment are an understanding of the true nature of reality and of one's own nature or true self.

As for reality, the information is readily available. We know that the universe has an antimaterial counterpart, that even the physical side is not made of matter but of frequency wave patterns. Learning this information and letting it sink in so that one appreciates this view of reality is what I call rational enlightenment. It's a major paradigm shift.

As for understanding one's own nature, we have some scientific findings, but not much yet really. However, by assembling several separate key discoveries into a system, I am able to illustrate one clear way of seeing how our consciousness works. I call this Sufi George's Dynamic Model of Consciousness (DMC). I provide a link to a Shockwave movie of the DMC.

The DMC looks at the antimaterial side of consciousness, beginning at the opposite pole from physical brain research. It begins where consciousness (awareness) actually resides, where it can be observed directly by observation. Why look for it in the brain when we already know where it is? Antimaterial reality is now a scientific reality, so why not base some assumptions on that instead of on Cartesian reality?

It is an obviously safe assumption that we are conscious, that we have that thing called consciousness. It doesn't have to be made of anything material to be real because some real things are antimaterial. We can assume we are examining consciousness because we simply and directly know that we are examining it. That's as safe as an assumption can get. It's directly intuitive rather than rational.

We don't need any of our physical senses to examine our consciousness. The part of ourselves that examines itself in this way is antimaterial, beyond the senses.

The DMC breaks down consciousness into separate components, and gives each a spatial body to help in visualizing the frequency wave fields that the components are made of. The core components are awareness, intuition and attention. The only moving part is attention. Awareness and intuition are motionless bodies that simply process the frequency waves that pass through them. Mostly, those frequency waves are selected by attention. We call this process experience.

All of this is obvious with a little introspection based on a current scientific understanding of the nature of reality.

The significant idea that the DMC produces is the idea of the generic human being, the skeleton, so to speak, that is identical within each of us, the ways in which we are all exactly the same. The generic human being is the human being minus its experience. That is, it's what's left if one has no experience at all to be aware of. It's what we call our true selves.

Experience originates outside of ourselves, and passes through us and then goes outside of ourselves again. It is a parade of patterns. It is not part of who we are. We can only experience it. We can't keep it, slow it down, stop it, repeat it, or do anything other than simply let it flow through us at its own pace.

So if one is searching for an understanding of one's true self, one needn't look at experience for the answer. Why not look for ourselves where we already know we are?

Who are we really? Well, when we strip away experience, all we have left is a consciousness system that is aware and prepared to process some signals. So who is that? That's the generic human being. That's every one of us. We are all identical in this way, and none of us can claim to own anything more because nothing else has permanence beyond the instant.

As the DMC illustrates, the signals each consciousness system, or, generic human being, receives only pass through its awareness. They are frequency waves that are all around us but invisible because they are spread out, expanded. Our attention can tune into them selectively, usually guided by the rational (Beta) mind and the imaginative (Alpha) mind.

Because of their shapes, attention first condenses these waves, and intuition then condenses them sharply. It is when the waves have been focused on one spot, like sunlight through a magnifying glass, that we are able to be aware of them. That spot, of course, is our awareness.

As the waves continue their travel, they go through a reversal of the process, and leave us once again as expanded and invisible wave fields.

These patterns must repeat, or else we could not have memory of them or persistence of reality. They would simply travel on and be gone. Memory and persistence are explained by the pattern that experience waves follow once they have been tuned into by attention. That pattern is a figure-eight or infinity loop.

This infinity loop has some remarkable features. Half of it is oriented to the material (Beta) world, and the other half to the imaginative (Alpha) world. Half of it is our future and half our past. It shows how our past becomes our future, which simply means that patterns we have experienced before are experienced again, such as the experience of remembering something or seeing something continue to exist.

Once we understand that our past becomes our future, we can create things in our future by planting them in our past. This is what we call creating our own reality and the DMC provides a clear way of understanding how it works. Such an understanding is very powerful, because with it one can literally change one's life in any way one wants. This is done by creating the patterns for the experiences one wants, a process I call building morphic robots.

Rupert Sheldrake's morphic field theory provides the foundation for this. He demonstrates that every physical reality has an antimaterial reality that contains the patterns which manifest in the physical world. These two realities interact, as if they're looped together. I present this as the DMC's experience loops.

We can see that it is easy to understand ourselves, using the DMC. There is some enlightenment here, too, because we can also understand everyone else, since they're the same as us. We can understand the generic human being in all of us.

As for experience, we can understand that no two people have the same. Each person's life is unique. We needn't wonder why this is so. Do we ask why there are so many different flowers? It's a law of nature; it's uniformly true for every one of us. It's obvious that it isn't going to change, not in Beta.

How does attention work? How does it select certain frequency wave fields and not others? We understand how our Beta mind directs our attention. If we decide to look at something, our attention simply goes there. We look at it. But our attention is also attracted to some fields without our conscious consent, seemingly at random. What's this?

This is resonance, powerful harmony between like frequencies. Like attracts like. We get more of what we have. Things build up, get stronger, and develop. Resonance is a basic principle of the physics of frequency waves.

We can understand the basic features of how experience works. The DMC is useful for tracking patterns through the process, noticing what happens to them and how they change each time they repeat.

After we understand reality, ourselves and our experience, we may still want that ultimate, mind-blowing experience that has been described in so many mystical and metaphysical traditions as Nirvana, Samadhi, or simply enlightenment.

Understanding is one thing, but actual first-hand experience of that understanding is needed to quench the desire for positive assurance. The combination of understanding and experience, of understanding the experience and experiencing the understanding so that they support each other, is the final reward.

This enlightenment experience has been difficult to get in the past. Today's scientists have made it readily available to almost anyone who is willing to prepare for it.

In lucid dreaming, one can design what one wants to experience. If one wants to experience the black void of awareness as being aware only of itself, this can be arranged in a lucid dream. One turns off experience and floats in what's left, pure awareness.

Lucid dreaming occurs in another reality, an alternate reality that follows different laws. It is the reality that has been described in so many different ways by so many different mystical traditions and religions. Today, though, we can study it like any other subject, and experience it by following proven exercises. Enlightenment no longer needs adjectives like cosmic or supreme. We do not need God to experience it.

The result of enlightenment is the certainty that we are

fundamentally nothing more (and nothing less) than awareness, awareness that has the ability to process experience wave fields. Awareness only experiences. It does not choose experiences. So awareness is not responsible for its experiences. Nor do experiences have any ultimate consequences.

There is a great liberation that comes with this realization. We know our permanent selves, so we know what dies and what survives at the time of physical death. We see life as a dream. As the song says, nothing seems to matter, my whole world could shatter, I don't care. Life becomes a thing to enjoy, to experiment with, to create.

We see our personality as a tool, not as who we are. We use it to interact with Beta reality. We change and develop it according to our wishes. We see that everyone's experience is unique, so we don't attempt to conform to outside standards except as they further our own purposes. Rather, we feel completely free to seek out new experiences, to live our lives in the fullest and most personally satisfying way.

The search for enlightenment now has a clear, uncluttered path. There is nothing to believe in, there is no mystery about it, and just about anyone can do it. This is a great time to be alive!

Our Consciousness of Mind and Body

We are aware of our pattern-processing mind and our body senses. The Dynamic Model of Consciousness shows us that both mind and body are experience patterns.

The DMC, with awareness at its center, surrounded by intuition, and banded by the ring of attention, is the system that delivers experience patterns to our awareness. So where do our mind and body fit in?

In the DMC, mind and body can be visualized as two little "moons" that orbit around the ball of attention. Recall that attention is a ball that orbits so fast, it makes a blur around the ball of intuition, a blur that looks like the rings of Saturn.

Although relatively insignificant in the overall model, mind and body tend to dominate attention because they are so close to the ball of attention. That is, their frequency waves reach attention swiftly and strongly.

Attention is aware of the frequency waves from the body ball when it tunes in to the waveband of 14 to 30 Hz (Beta).

It is aware of the mind ball when it spreads to 8 to 13 Hz (Alpha). We can observe the difference simply by noting how much faster-paced our Beta experience is compared to our Alpha experience in the slower frequency waveband.

Our body experience consists of processing patterns that we normally consider as material reality. However, since all experience comes from patterns (frequency wave field patterns, or morphic fields), this is an illusion, an interpretation of patterns in our awareness.

Our ability to lift up patterns in Beta, move them around "physically," kick them across the room, is all happening as awareness of frequency wave patterns. Face it, the only thing we can do in so-called material reality is experience it in our awareness.

In mind, we do the same thing, except we recognize that we are dealing with anti-material patterns like thoughts, daydreams and imaginings. These are more relaxed realities, as indicated by the slower frequency waveband.

The word "mind" is widely misused to mean anything from a thought-processor to consciousness itself. Let's get it straight. Mind processes patterns. The function of mind is to make sense of experience patterns.

Without mind, we have a consciousness system that is open to unfiltered patterns. These enter attention, pass through intuition and are experienced in awareness. Under these circumstances, the patterns may be noted, but they will not have personal significance or importance. They lack personal meaning.

Mind, then, has the task of processing experience patterns and determining what might be called the truth in them.

Mind has four modes for producing truth—blind faith, speculation, reason, and science. The quality of truth produced depends on the mode used, and that's a matter of experience and skill.

Truth produced by mind is necessarily relative since every one of us produces it in our unique fashion, from our own perspective on our own experience, using modes according to our own skill level. The quality of truth produced by mind is never as satisfying as the immediate, indisputable truth of our awareness, intuition and attention.

Mind goes through complicated processes to determine or create truth. But the truths of our three basic components of consciousness are apparent without process.

However, mind is a reality that we need to deal with. It insists on being satisfied on questions of truth, almost regardless of how that is achieved.

We can judge our own truth according to whether our mind produced it by blind faith (seeing is believing), speculation (unverifiable imagination), reason (disciplined rational thought process) or understanding of scientific truth (rational thought verified by experimentation, mind's highest achievement).

The ideal truth is one that matches our immediate truths (awareness, intuition and attention) with scientific proof and explanation. Today, we have this from our sciences, especially physics, and this is the information that has led to the development of the Dynamic Model of Consciousness.

Mind and body senses are both creations of our attention system, developed over long stretches of experience.

Attention created mind to produce truth, and senses to produce Beta experience of that truth.

Mind and body senses are both tuned in to the same experience patterns. When our attention is tuned in to Beta, we experience the patterns as material realities. When tuned in to Alpha, we experience them as anti-material patterns. But the patterns are the same. Only our perspective changes.

My Life Is Such a Mess

We say it; we hear it all the time. "My life is such a mess. Is it really true that I created this mess myself?"

I? Which "I" are we referring to? Ego or awareness?

The ego is an accumulation of "truth" about ourselves. We have built it up from childhood, mostly from the observations of others about us.

It's truth like, "I am the boss of this entity," but it only has that as an idea.

There's a lot in life that is beyond the influence of the ego.

It's truth like, "I am the whole thing, all of this entity," but to preserve this myth, ego has to rule out, keep out, other experiences like dreams or intuitions.

Most of us were careless about the truth that we developed for our egos. Like children, we built our egos haphazardly, not knowing any better. After all, children is exactly what we were.

We face the problem of believing in our egos, and that gets shaky because we know down deep that it's a dishonest product.

When we have a basic mistrust of our egos because of dishonesty with ourselves in creating them, one of the consequences is that we have to live dishonestly.

It is a lie that ego is the entire entity. It is a lie that the ego is in control of the entity. And with such lies in the foundation of the ego, it's easy to attach many lesser lies to it.

The mistake in our thinking is that when we wonder, "was I responsible for creating my new reality?" we are thinking about the wrong "I." It was not the "I" of the ego that was responsible. In fact, the ego has very little creative ability.

Yes, we are responsible, but "we" is our attention system and all that is in it, which includes the ego as one thing.

If we don't correct this mistake, then we'll try to create or change our reality by using the ego, and that's not where it's at. Correct this mistake and we'll be more effective at creating our reality.

Our messy life was created by the attention we paid to our experience patterns. Attention involves resonance which adds life to experience patterns and assures that they will manifest in our future.

When we control what our attention is resonating with, then we can reshape our experience patterns and clean up our mess.

We can only do that by centering ourselves not in the ego but in our attention system itself. We must be aware of our attention at work, monitor its activities, and regulate what it resonates with. We must deny resonance with patterns we don't want, and build resonance with patterns we do want.

We must stop paying so much attention to our egos and pay attention to attention itself.

Figuring Out Your Ego

Ego is our front line identity, the part of us that is out there interacting with everyone else.

Ego is our prince of morphic robots. What created it, what is it made of, and who is it really? Is it responsible for creating our reality?

When we are children, we know who we are, even if we can't put it into words. Then, who we are is put into words for us, and it's not the same as we thought.

Every time we hear something about who we are, it adds to our Beta mind knowledge of ourselves, and this builds into an ego, or our idea of who we are supposed to be in Beta.

We will feel like we are the ego, that it's us out there on the front lines facing the unknown at every turn, fighting for survival one way or another. We'll believe it, with only an ache from the lie.

Ego is a tool, a user interface, and we can step back and manage it for best effect. Compared to not doing this, the results can be amazing. Wonderful things can be accomplished quickly.

There are several possibilities for identifying ourselves. The first, everybody's first, is the ego. The ego is made of ideas and concepts and exists only in the mind of the person. The mind is just part of a person.

It's hard to understand ego without first understanding mind. Understanding mind can be confusing, too. Like, truth is whatever the mind creates as truth. Truth can be made of anything from childish belief to scientific discovery. If the mind says to our attention, this is truth, and there's no argument about it, that that is truth.

The ego is truth about ourselves. We have built it up out of various ideas.

It's truth like "I am the boss of this entity," but it only has that as an idea. There's a lot in life that is beyond the influence of the ego.

It's truth like "I am the whole thing, all of this entity," but it has to constantly try to rule out, keep out, other things, like dreams or intuitions.

The Human Experience of Reality

For the time that we are human, we have two major areas of concern.

One is living our lives in physical reality, and ultimately this is a question of finding the purpose of our lives or answering the question, why am I alive?

The other is exploring what is beyond physical reality, and for most this boils down to a concern with what happens after death.

Understanding what physical reality is, as well as what it isn't, helps us to gain a perspective that can help a great deal in wrestling with the questions of life's purpose and sequels.

Why are we alive? Well, before we answer that, we have to answer this question: where are we alive?

Our environment has a whole lot to do with why we are in it. Let's begin at the beginning of our environment.

We have fresh ideas on the creation of the physical universe. Instead of assuming that physical reality is all there is, which raises the impossible questions of what came before it and what is outside of it, we now can view the physical universe as a subset in a much greater universe filled with various dimensions of reality.

There are certain prerequisites for the creation of physical reality, prerequisites that would apply to the creation of any dimension of reality.

The first prerequisite is a universe as an entity made up of patterns of possibility that have awareness. Unless something is possible, it can't exist. Unless there is awareness, there is no experience of existence and therefore no existence.

The second is attention. Without the limitation of attention, the universe is omniscient, aware of every possibility simultaneously, unable to experience anything specific or separate. Without attention, there are no individuals in the universe. There is only the blur of chaos.

The origin of awareness is the only mystery in the universe. There is no doubt about the existence of awareness, however. It is by far our most immediate and intimate reality.

Attention is inherent in possibilities themselves, simply because there is more than one possibility in the universe. This multiplicity divides awareness into units of attention as small as subatomic units, as far as we know now.

It is essential to understand that we humans are high level systems. Our awareness is made up of the same awareness as that in subatomic units, which have combined into systems, which have combined into greater systems, and so on until we have the extremely complicated phenomenon called human awareness.

It's easier to grasp this idea of very complicated systems developing from tiny bits when we count the billions of cells that make up the human body. Our bodies are full of complicated systems, all cellular at root, and while we may think of ourselves as single entities, we are also made of nothing but individual cells.

When we marvel at the complicated abilities and characteristics of our awareness, we must realize that this, too, is made up of billions of bits working in systems.

Nothing has changed fundamentally. It's still bits. In created systems, nothing is fundamentally new, except for the effect of systems being greater than the sum of their parts.

Thus everything, material and non-material, is made up of that sparse reality we call non-material aware possibilities. With this realization, let's review the creation of the physical universe.

Morphic fields, patterns with awareness, exist in universal consciousness as possibilities. The patterns for physical reality are possible systems, possible as cooperative interactions. The patterns are aware of themselves and interact with each other through resonance.

High level attention systems, morphic fields which we can call entities, are responsible for assembling the systems of morphic field patterns required for the experience called physical reality.

These entities interrelate morphic fields in such a way that they create patterns for a new source of experience. They have an ambitious and complicated dream-physical reality. There is no such thing as physical material to create it with, but this isn't essential since the objective is experience, not matter.

The dominant peculiarities of the physical universe are to be space and time, nonmaterial morphic field realities.

The plan is to build a cosmic theater in which attention systems can experience location and continuity, neither of which is available without the appropriate morphic fields.

All of the needed morphic fields establish the relationships necessary for physical reality to exist. Time and space begin within the limits of the patterns of physical reality.

There is a Big Bang, establishing the finite beginning necessary for "real" time and space to exist.

In real time, the universe has a beginning and an end at singularities that form a boundary to space-time and at which the laws of science break down. But in imaginary time, there are no singularities or boundaries. So maybe what we call imaginary time is really more basic, and what we call real is just an idea that we invent to help us describe what we think the universe is like, says Stephen Hawking in *A Brief History of Time*.

From a fraction of a second after this point and on to the present, science has figured out just about everything else, and here we are.

As individuals, we are attention systems. An attention system is awareness that is limited by attention to a certain field of experience or to resonance with a certain dimension of morphic fields.

Our attention system is substantially restricted to experience within the morphic fields of space and time. If we didn't have the limited condition of space, we couldn't be somewhere. Even if we found a place, without time we wouldn't experience existence as continuous, we couldn't stay put.

Space and time (and the limitation of attention to those patterns) are what make it possible to have a human body. Space gives us the opportunity to focus our location, and time gives us the opportunity to experience continuity.

Thus, when the physical universe was created, it was not something more—it was something less. It was a subset of patterns, and a restriction of attention to that subset.

All that happened, really, is that morphic fields developed into new systems and our attention was restricted to this subset of the possibilities in the universe.

Just as we can temporarily accept that a novel or a movie or a dream is real, so we accept physical reality as real. They are all the same in the sense that we only experience them.

A dimension is a set of morphic fields or patterns designed to occupy attention more or less exclusively. Morphic fields of a dimension passing through awareness create the experience of a dimension of reality.

Our physical dimension has its own laws, contained in its own patterns. The two most important laws are space and time.

Both of these laws have been shown not to exist in the same way in the subatomic or fourth dimension of modern physicists. Time there becomes relative and space curves around itself and interchanges with time.

Space and time are not fixed realities except in the morphic field patterns for dimensions such as our physical universe.

Nor does our space and time necessarily have any relationship to the space and time of another dimension which may also have such laws.

In order to have space and time, there must be patterns that create the experience of those perceptions when they pass through awareness.

Thus, we can escape space and time by focusing our attention on a different dimension that doesn't have them.

Eternity is not a matter of endless time. It is a matter of no time. The universe as an entity is eternal, not in relation to our physical time, but because all is always everything at once. When we talk about time as we know it, we are limiting our discussion to our three-dimensional physical world.

Stephen LaBerge showed that a ten-second time span in dream reality is the same as a ten-second time span in physical reality, given that the dreamer has simultaneous awareness of both dimensions.

Yet, any dreamer knows that time is different in dream reality. Some dreams seem to last for hours or days, when the dreamer has only napped for several minutes. Time, then, while it can mimic time as we know it in physical reality, is very flexible in dream reality.

And we know that space is quite different in dream reality. Our dream environment can change radically in an instant, a phenomenon that is impossible in three-dimensional reality, and which calls to mind the behavior of paired electrons in Bell's Theorem.

These are examples of how time and space can follow different laws in another dimension of reality. In fact, these fit very comfortably with the descriptions of time and space in the fourth dimension by modern physics, leading to the conclusion that dream reality is a more basic reality than the physical world.

The universe as an entity is every possibility coexisting in simultaneous awareness, without any limitation of attention. It is a universe where every possibility is homogenized with every other, and can be experienced as a boundless, timeless aware blackness where nothing has yet been individualized or created.

Attention is a division of this universe into limited attention systems.

Each of the tiniest subatomic particles has individual awareness, is a tiny attention system.

These tiny attention systems group themselves into greater systems, and this is the creation process of higher level attention systems.

Our own high level attention systems, our individualized selves, consist of sub-systems. We may not be consciously aware of other aspects of our attention systems, but nonetheless they operate in their own full awareness.

What many call the unconscious mind is not unconscious at all (nor is it mind); it is one of the sub-systems of our attention system, as is our ordinary consciousness.

Thus, our attention system is much more involved than our usual waking conscious awareness would suggest. Our attention can focus on different sub-systems within the general pattern of our attention system or individualized selves.

Dreams are an example of focusing attention on a sub-system that many call the unconscious. The point is, while our attention is focused on it, it is not unconscious at all; it is conscious and we experience it directly.

Conversely, in the usual dream state, the sub-system we call ordinary waking consciousness could be called unconscious because we are then not aware of it.

So, all of our attention sub-systems are fully aware. We experience their awareness when we focus our attention on them.

The breakthrough experiments with lucid dreaming by Stephen LaBerge have established to the satisfaction of a skeptical scientific community that dream reality does exist as an independent dimension of reality.

Dream reality has its own laws, many of which differ from physical laws. However, experience of dream reality is entirely as real as any experience in the physical dimension, and lucid dreaming has been described by many as "more real than real."

Lucid dreaming is the first technique for experience of another dimension of reality to be proven by science. Many more are as yet unproven but have strong anecdotal support.

Lucid dream experiments have proven that we can focus our attention on two sub-systems at the same time, so it really is a matter of focusing attention and not a question of whether a sub-system is conscious or unconscious.

By the way, LaBerge's spin-off discovery of awareness of two dimensions at the same time can explain strange things like déjà-vu, night paralysis, hallucinations, ghosts, visions, and a multitude of phenomena that involve experiencing from two sources at one time.

Our environment, in specific terms, is our attention system and its subsystems. This is, usually, the only reality we experience. Our attention system is focused on our personal universe.

Of course, this is speaking in usual terms. There is the open possibility of experiencing systems beyond our personal attention systems, deliberately using techniques that manipulate the scope of our attention.

Another law of the physical universe is the life cycle. The human experience, for example, is designed to conclude at some point.

Life cycle is the ultimate solution to the condition of being locked into a particular focus of attention of three-dimensional reality.

I need convince no one of the fact that three-dimensional reality has the quality of seeming to be all that there is.

While everyone experiences various kinds of hints otherwise, and while some people deliberately refocus their attention to other dimensions, most of us see death as the only way out.

Were it not for the law of life cycle, the three-dimensional world would be a trap. If the physical body didn't die, we would be locked into it until we found an escape or until the physical universe itself reached the end of its life cycle.

The law of life cycle makes it clear that three-dimensional reality is only one of the dimensions that we are to experience.

However, it is the dimension of immediate interest, so let's continue examining it.

The bulk of our experience of physical reality comes through our sensory system.

Intricately designed, each sense passes on data it gets from interacting with other patterns, resonating with other morphic fields.

Each sense has its special morphic field pattern, and each is specifically suited for interactions with patterns in the physical world.

What would our experience be like without our sensory system?

We would be aware; we would have intuition, attention, mind, emotion. We would be completely the same as now except that fresh data from our senses would be missing. We'd perhaps be focusing our attention on some other dimension, or perhaps looking for a way to get back into physical reality.

As noted elsewhere, we would still be able to see and hear because these result from intuition.

This, of course, describes the "afterlife." It is perfectly reasonable to say that after death, one's attention is focused on dream reality. But let's get back to life.

Our personal field of consciousness is full of distinct realities, made of systems of morphic fields. We cannot be aware of very many of them at the same time, usually, because we usually have our attention focused rather narrowly on our particular life experience of the moment.

In the case of what we call physical realities, objective things, a morphic field interacts with its physical counterpart through the process of resonance, and both the morphic and physical realities change content through a looping interaction, always attempting to reflect each other identically in the face of constant change.

Resonance is an interaction of waves, as in electrical energy waves, and electrical energy waves provide a good metaphor because they are an actual example of resonance when they interact.

Material particles have a probability of existing in space—they have a location; and in time they persist. The reality of waves is non-material and they do not occupy a fixed position in space, though they travel through time. The reality of awareness is independent of both time and space. This gives us a glimpse into the systemic stages or dimensions that result in matter.

First there are morphic fields with awareness, which express in time as waves, which express in time and space as matter.

A morphic field is a pattern. As with all patterns in the universe, it has awareness. As with all patterns, it is part of the network of the universe, ultimately interconnected with every other pattern.

Every pattern interconnects with other patterns through interacting waves. This is resonance.

We know from the example of electrical energy that resonance can vary in degrees of harmony (frequency and polarity). Some wave interactions are opposing, others are attractive. Two magnets illustrate this.

Polarity accounts for the way different morphic fields "get along" with each other. We are all familiar with instant likes and dislikes of things, people, events, etc. These are the actions of polarized resonance.

Given that each of us has a personal reality environment described by our own morphic field systems, for any individual there will be things in life that are simply disharmonious, that cannot be fit in, and other things that harmonize, that complement and add to our experience.

Force-fitting disharmonious morphic fields into one's life results in static and sparks, experienced as discomfort, conflict and disease. Resonance is a reliable guide through life for identifying those morphic fields that will build harmoniously in the environment of patterns one has to begin with.

Morphic fields can exist without a physical counterpart (most do), as in the case of certain thoughts and other realities that are exclusively in awareness.

Every reality in consciousness can be understood as a morphic field. We already understand realities in terms of nested systems, where lesser realities combine to create greater realities. We can now understand realities as relationships of lesser and greater morphic fields.

Physicists tell us that all patterns are interrelated in such a complex fashion that the universe can be seen as a single entity. The universe itself is a morphic field, made up of seemingly endless relationships of nested lesser morphic fields.

While our experience is that of individualized, separate attention systems, we are each inseparably in and of the universe and everything in it. While the universe itself may be a lone entity, we as subsets have a lot of company within that entity.

The field of universal consciousness is filled with morphic fields containing all of the possibilities for experience or reality. As an inseparable attribute of awareness, intuition can interact with or relate to any morphic field in the universe.

Since the physical universe is a non-material dimension of patterns experienced in awareness, it makes a lot of sense to approach ordinary reality first in terms of its morphic fields.

In fact, we do this routinely. A skyscraper exists first as an inspiration, develops into a detailed pattern that exists only in awareness (although it may be recorded on paper), and involves large numbers of other morphic fields manipulated in mind before it can materialize as a physical pattern.

What determines exactly which morphic fields become parts of our immediate reality? In simple terms, it is the polarity and intensity of resonance.

As human beings, we each have our own morphic field, an aware entity that contains our experience of self. Further, our morphic fields make up larger morphic fields, such as groups, societies, etc.

Thus, we each have an environment of specific morphic fields, all resonating in substantial harmony. Each of these morphic fields is itself aware, and combined there is a general or higher level of awareness. Humanity itself is a rapidly developing morphic field that should be of great interest to us.

It is our intuition that enables our awareness to resonate with specific morphic fields.

Since our awareness is constantly filled with the resonance of patterns flowing through intuition, it is possible to experience any morphic field that is accessible by intuition, that is, any morphic field in the universe.

In practical terms, however, we will resonate with those experience patterns that are harmonious with our environment. If we want something more or something different, we must deliberately generate resonance with a selected morphic field by holding it in awareness, using attention to do this.

Who are we, then? We are aware entities resonating with experience patterns held in a personal universe and also with patterns reaching us from outside of our personal universe.

What is our purpose? In a real sense, our purpose is what we choose it to be. However, we cannot choose experience patterns with disharmonious resonance without wrecking ourselves. So, there are definite limitations to possible purposes in our lives.

Translating this into more practical terms, we are permanently existing fields of consciousness temporarily trapped in the material theater. Our purpose is limited to what we can actually do, given our abilities, talents, skills, circumstances and opportunities.

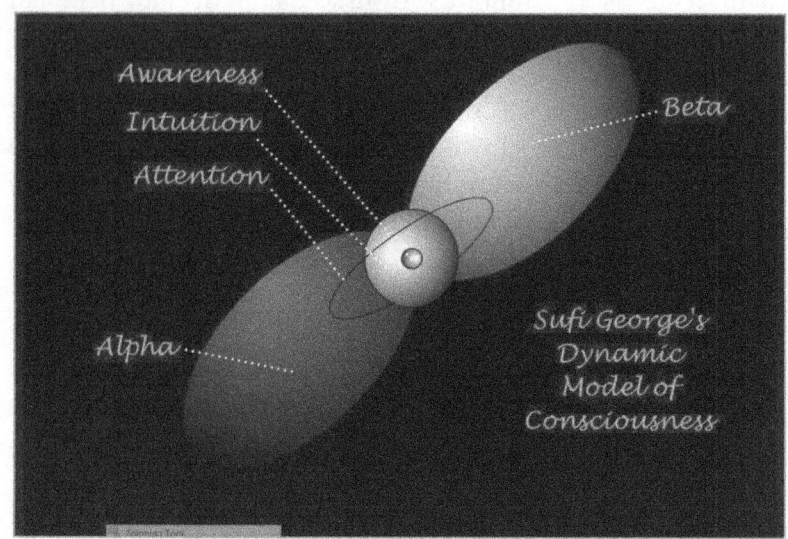

A Shockwave movie of Sufi George's Dynamic Model of Consciousness can be seen at http://sufigeorge.net/dmc270.swf.

The Components of Consciousness

We live in a lucky century. For the first time in our known history, we can understand much about the basic nature of our own consciousness. Drawing on the work of particle physicists and other scientists, and on my own 40 years of consciousness exploration, I have designed the Dynamic Model of Consciousness (DMC). This model explains what our consciousness is and how it works, and its accuracy can be confirmed in our own experience.

The DMC gives us a completely new perspective on the nature of our reality, with an understanding that is practical, rationally satisfying, and intuitively accurate. I'll describe and explain the DMC, and give you ways to see it at work within yourself.

This is not merely interesting; it is powerful. Understanding how our consciousness works gives us the power to create the reality we experience. Our first step to understanding consciousness is to break it down into its components. Later, we can reassemble the components into a consciousness system.

The first component is awareness, our fundamental reality. Looked at by itself, awareness is aware of very little, only of itself as an entity, and of course, aware of being aware.

Intuition is the next component. Despite its popular mystique, intuition has only one function in the model. It focuses patterns of experience so that they become vivid or real. Intuition can receive patterns from any direction.

The practical heart of consciousness is our attention system. It is the only component that moves under our direction, and it works like an antenna or tuner that focuses or limits our experience. Without attention, we would not only be aware of all experience patterns at the same time (chaos), but we would have no sense of individual identity.

Awareness, intuition and attention are the heart of our consciousness system. They process experience patterns and give us our sense of living reality. Aside from these three, all else is outside of us, as experience.

Awareness can be visualized as a clear glass marble at the core of the model, enclosed or surrounded by a larger crystal ball which is intuition.

Attention can be visualized as a ring around intuition, like the rings around the planet Saturn. In the model, experience patterns pass through attention, intuition and awareness, and that is how we get to enjoy experiences.

The important point to grasp at this stage is the basic difference between who we are and what we experience. We are awareness. As awareness, we know only two things: that we are aware, and that we exist. Everything else comes to us from the outside as experience. We pay attention to experience patterns, and intuition brings them alive in our awareness.

Technically, experience patterns are frequency wave interference field patterns, or morphic fields. This is not at all as mysterious as it may sound. Just think of the frequency waves from TV stations filling the space around us. They are invisible until they are tuned into and focused into a meaningful image that we can experience. Very much the same thing is happening in our consciousness system. The frequency waves of experience patterns are tuned into by our attention, focused into a meaningful reality by our intuition, and experienced as real in our awareness.

In the DMC, intuition is visualized as a crystal ball because this illustrates how light waves are focused down to a point in the center, the same thing we see when we hold a magnifying glass under the sun and make a hot spot. We aren't aware of experience patterns until they are focused down by intuition.

Because of the lens effect of a crystal ball, we can visualize experience patterns entering the ball of intuition, getting focused down to where we are aware of them as intense realities in the center point of awareness, and then seeing them get defocused or expanded back to their original form on their way out the other side of the ball. This is how we experience anything and everything, other than our awareness itself.

To illustrate this further, let's talk about the common experience of seeing light. Physically, light rays (frequency waves) enter our eyes, but are stopped by the retina at the back of the eyeball. From there, the waves are converted into electrical and chemical signals, and travel through the brain in darkness. Where is the light? Also, we see light in dreams. Where does this light come from? These mysteries are explained by understanding that all experience patterns are resolved or focused by intuition and are then experienced in awareness.

By approaching our experience from the viewpoint of consciousness, rather than from our physical and mental senses, we can understand how we are able to have experience.

Attention

In our discussion so far of the Dynamic Model of Consciousness, we've looked at the three major components: awareness, intuition and attention.

Awareness simply is. It is aware, and it is aware that it is an aware entity. There's nothing more to it than that, but of course, without awareness there isn't anything at all.

Intuition is very a different thing than we ordinarily suppose. It works like a lens, focusing experience patterns down to intense realities in our awareness, and then defocusing them again.

Visualizing the Dynamic Model of Consciousness, we see awareness as a glass marble in the center of the model, surrounded or enclosed by a crystal ball that represents intuition.

Around the ball of intuition is a ring, like the rings around the planet Saturn. Let's examine this important ring more closely to see what it is doing for us.

The ring represents attention. Now, we can be aware of experience patterns without attention, because patterns can enter the ball of intuition from any direction. However, this access to all patterns at once can be chaotic.

It is attention that restricts or limits our experience so we can be aware of only certain experiences at a time, instead of everything at once.

Visualizing the model, we see that the ring of attention is really a blur resulting from the very rapid orbiting of a ball. This ball is actually attention, but the ring it forms is important in its own way.

The ring works like an antenna. It has a flat plane, and only those experience patterns that are in line with this plane can be accessed by attention.

The ring works like an antenna, and the ball of attention works like a tuner, further limiting the patterns of experience that we are aware of at a given time.

Visualize an experience pattern on the plane of the attention ring. See it coming from a certain direction, from another person, for example. As the attention ball orbits, it will "click" with this pattern on each orbit, thus tuning in to it.

The pattern, then, flows into the ring of attention. Because this ring is flat, the pattern is forced into a wedge shape as it travels from the outside of the ring to the inside. This means that the pattern is focused or intensified by attention before it reaches the ball of intuition.

Intuition, then, focuses a pattern that is already somewhat focused by attention, and when the pattern reaches awareness, it has greater focus or intensity than patterns that arrive through intuition directly.

This is why the patterns that travel first through attention are dominant in our awareness, dominant over experiences that arrive directly through intuition.

We know from brainwave research that our attention is receptive to experience patterns, frequency wave field patterns, in four wavebands. That is, our brainwaves measure in four different wavebands according to the type of reality we are aware of.

For attention to experience material reality it must be tuned between 14 and 30 Hz (cycles per second). For daydream reality, it must be tuned from 8 to 13 Hz. For dream reality, it's 4 to 7 Hz. And for lucid dream reality, a combination of these first three, it must be tuned from 0.5 to 3 Hz.

These wavebands are called Beta, Alpha, Theta and Delta, respectively.

We know that three of these are antimaterial—daydreams, common dreams and lucid dreams. However, most people doubt that Beta, material reality, is also made of antimaterial frequency wave patterns.

With just a moment's thought, though, we can realize that our experience of Beta reality consists of receiving light waves, sound waves, vibratory waves, etc. Thus, we can understand that Beta reality is equally antimaterial.

Remember, when we experience something, anything, all that is really happening is that experience patterns (frequency wave field interference patterns) are passing through our awareness.

It's all patterns. None of it is actually material. Materiality is just one more experience that we're aware of, and mostly, we're aware of the experience we are paying attention to.

Where Is Our Attention Focused?

What we pay attention to is what we experience.

Attention is what limits our awareness to a certain selection of experiences. We know this with certainty because we experience it directly.

We also know from directing our attention ("paying" attention) that we are in charge of focusing our attention when and if we want to be. Otherwise, attention does its thing without control, receiving whatever experience patterns enter into it.

Our attention covers two universes, sometimes more. The usual two universes are the ones we live in all the time, Beta reality and Alpha reality.

Beta reality is our material world. Alpha reality is our antimaterial world, full of ideas, thoughts and daydreams.

Is our attention more focused on our Alpha universe or our Beta universe? Are we mainly dreamers or doers? Are we mainly stressed or relaxed? Are we mainly thinkers or builders?

We have three vital signs that we can check, and they answer such questions about how our attention is spread between Beta and Alpha.

It's interesting to realize that these vital sign checks are directly connected with where our attention is focused, especially considering that we can decide how to focus our attention and produce a deliberate result.

To make this check of your attention's vital signs, draw on a piece of paper three intersecting lines like a snowflake, all crossing together in the middle.

Sketch a skimpy horizontal line right across the middle, through the center of the snowflake. This line divides Beta and Alpha experience.

Above the snowflake, write "Beta" and below write "Alpha." At the 12:00 position on the snowflake, write "Future," at 2:00 "Stress," 4:00 "Antimatter," 6:00 "Past," 8:00 "Relax," and 10:00 "Matter."

Now we can draw a picture of how our attention is distributed in these ways by plotting points on the lines and "connecting the dots."

This is a simple picture, of course, but it reveals the pattern of how our attention is distributed, and that's interesting to think about.

The first vital sign is our position on the line of time. We can see if we are mainly in Alpha or in Beta reality by checking our time line position.

Is our experience (and that's what's passing through our little window of NOW) mostly memories of the past? Or are we mostly thinking about our plans for the future? The past is Alpha and the future is Beta. Simple, huh?

Which is more important to our experience, planning the future or reviewing the past? Are our most important experiences material or are they experienced within? If we had to choose between giving up our past and giving up our future, which would we choose?

Now, to refine this, since we are all partly Alpha and partly Beta, think about how Beta you are and how Alpha you are. Then put two dots down to show this on the time line.

The second vital sign is a simple stress-relaxation check. The more stressed we are, the more in Beta. The more relaxed, the more in Alpha.

We just observe how fast or slow our attention is running. Beta reality tunes in to brainwaves of 14 to 30 Hz, much faster than the 8 to 13 Hz of Alpha reality. We know the difference from experience. Material reality is hard work, and Alpha reality is just day dreamy.

When we're busy builders out there in Beta reality, our attention races. And when we kick back and daydream, our attention purrs.

So we put two dots to show how stressed we are in Beta and how relaxed we are in Alpha, giving more weight to whichever is more prominent in our experience.

Are we materialistic? Are we creative artists? We can learn our matter-antimatter position with the third vital sign. Beta is matter, Alpha is antimatter.

We can take these checks according to how we frame our thinking, such as our answers in general or our answers for a particular day or moment.

Now, we can draw a chubby picture that connects the points and we will have a visible picture of our attention and how it's distributed.

We can use our results to name an attention type, such as Alpha-Beta-Alpha type to represent time, stress and matter parameters.

There are four ways we can see where our attention is mainly focused. I've tucked another one in here.

1. We can check our brainwaves and see if they are tuned into Beta, 14-30 Hz, or to Alpha, 8-13 Hz. Well, we probably can't do that for ourselves, but we know that there is equipment that can do it. This will show the overall Beta-Alpha relationship.

2. We can check our timeline position. Are we resonating more with patterns from the past (Alpha)? Or with patterns for the future (Beta)?

3. We can check our stress level. Beta reality, with its faster frequencies, is more stressful to experience. Alpha, at slower frequencies, is more relaxed and peaceful.

4. We can check our matter-antimatter position. Are we resonating mainly with material things? Or with nonmaterial patterns?

Intuition Demystified

Picture a clear glass marble. That's awareness. Now, wrap a clear glass ball around it so the marble is in the middle of the ball. That's intuition.

Now put a Saturn ring around it, and that's our attention field. It's actually a ball orbiting the intuition ball so fast that it blurs and makes the ring.

The Dynamic Model of Consciousness shows that our awareness depends on our intuition for receiving experience patterns. Awareness is totally covered over by intuition. This means that any frequency signals headed for awareness need to pass through intuition to get there.

That is, our intuition is what processes the frequency wave patterns received from attention and other sources, and resolves them into the reality we are aware of. It produces the same result you would expect from the lens effect of a crystal ball resolving light rays down to an intense point in the center.

The model also shows the relationship between intuition

and attention. Since intuition's field is in contact with the entire inner circle of attention, it can receive everything attention has to offer. Because of attention's flat ring shape, patterns entering from the outside are compacted as they flow toward the smaller radius of the inner part of the ring.

This forces an increase in resonance, and explains why patterns received through attention dominate our awareness, compared to patterns received through intuition directly. Intuition is exposed to a much larger field outside of attention, and it can receive experience patterns from beyond Alpha and Beta realities. Since the ball of intuition has surfaces in all directions, it can receive patterns from any direction.

Our intuition is so close to us, so right in front of our faces, that we usually overlook it. Intuition is processing every one of our experience patterns, handing us our every experience. It is our eyes and our ears in every dimension, including ordinary Beta reality.

Look at the experience that's passing through our window of NOW. We're sitting here, and that's awareness, that's the center, that's our true self. Experience patterns are going through this window. Attention has picked most of them out. Attention boosted their resonance, and now intuition gets them.

As our experience patterns pass through intuition, they are resolved or focused into meaningful experiences. Their level of meaningfulness comes from the power of their resonance. The stronger the resonance, the more we find meaning, purpose, emotion and reality in the patterns.

Attention is usually busy with the patterns it gets from body and mind, its two moons orbiting it on the same plane as the ring. These experiences dominate our attention. We are completely accustomed to intuition's focusing and delivery of our physical Beta reality. We don't even see it happening any more.

What we do see happening sometimes is intuition resonating with experience patterns that come from outside the ring of attention. These are less strong because they haven't passed through the ring of attention. Because of that, we often just dismiss them.

Since we get most of our experience from attention, when we get these outside signals, they feel unusual, less real, and sometimes spooky.

We can actually see a working model that demonstrates very clearly how intuition receives frequency wave patterns and turns them into meaningful reality. Our model is a TV set. It receives experience patterns out of a field of frequency waves and tunes them into a clear picture. With sound, yet. At the level of frequency wave activity, this is exactly what attention and intuition do, except they come with a screen guaranteed forever.

The DMC shows our experience patterns reaching awareness through our ring of attention, our intuition condensing or resolving them into a meaningful picture, and awareness experiencing them. What we normally call intuition is a pattern that enters intuition from anywhere except through the attention ring. Such a pattern has not been through attention and so it does not arrive in awareness with the boost in resonance that attention gives to a pattern.

So, we can realize that most of our experience patterns come from body and mind, both being sharply resolved by intuition. These sharply defined patterns command our awareness. When the weaker patterns come directly through intuition, they are easy to ignore; they are not commanding. Even when they have very strong resonance patterns, they can be shrugged off because of their unfamiliarity. However, such strong patterns have strong meaning.

It's the same thing—resonance equals meaning, purpose, emotion, reality. That's what gives intuitive patterns their importance.

A Guided Tour of Our Consciousness

Welcome to our tour of the highlights of our consciousness!

Most folks who come here to our consciousness museum say they understand themselves a lot better after this tour. I hope you enjoy the same experience today!

The Highlights of Consciousness tour gives you the big picture of our daily consciousness. If you feel like we're going too fast and rushing past too many things today, that's just because it's the Highlights Tour and this job of being your guide keeps me hopping.

First Stop—Awareness

Let's begin the tour right where we are, right in the center of everything. This is our first exhibit, awareness. Kind of looks like a little glass marble, don't it? Well, it talks. Here, I'll push the button.

"At the center or core of consciousness is me, awareness. Awareness is who or what we really are. Awareness is our first and most basic reality.

"I am aware of my awareness itself. I am aware that it is I who am aware. Those two things, and that's it as far as our true self goes.

"Now, if I include what's outside of me, then I'm aware of more than my awareness. I am aware of my experience. These are two different things. My awareness is the real me and my experience comes from out there.

"I can't see any other reality. That really covers it all. There's the aware me and there's my experience and that's it." (Click)

Get it? You see, experience is all there is out there because that's what everything boils down to. Reality is just our experience, what we are aware of.

What was that? Where does awareness come from? Just a second, there's a button here for this. Technical button, for people like you who ask questions.

"Today, science teaches us that the universe is a network of nonmaterial patterns. These patterns are frequency wave fields or frequency wave interference patterns. Our model of consciousness, here, shows that these patterns exhibit awareness.

The "basic building block" of any reality is a pattern that is aware of itself, that is, of its existence, processes and purpose. An example is the pattern of a line, a one-dimensional reality that knows it's the pattern for a line."

I can turn this off if you want. Leave it on? You're swallowing that about a line that's aware of itself? Well, okay.

"Simple one-dimensional awareness exists as a frequency wave, a line. These lines make up field patterns when they interfere or intermingle with each other.

"From this simple one-dimensional field pattern, complex patterns develop as interference wave patterns, and interactions of these wave fields in all directions create awareness of three dimensions. This is our awareness having experience." (Click)

Around here, we like to call awareness, here, our little window of NOW. Gives you the feeling that you're stopped in time and time is flowing by in front of you instead.

Next Stop—Intuition

Our most awesome, is that how they say it? a-a-awesome? Anyway, this is the famous intuition. Looks like a crystal ball, don't it? Anyways, this ball wraps around the awareness ball. Forget it, I'll hit the button.

"I see the difference between the true self, awareness, and the part that delivers experience, which is me, intuition.

"I am what makes sense out of all those frequency wave patterns out there and turn them into experience, a movie that awareness can live in.

"It's because of me, intuition, that awareness can see, hear, sense, or have any kind of experience. I am interpreting billions of waves into experience patterns just for awareness."

Is that enough of that one? You want more?

"I make those experience patterns just come alive. How do I do this? I receive the patterns from any direction. The patterns travel right through me. Because I am like a ball of crystal, a lens, you might say, the patterns get focused down to vivid, meaningful images by the time they reach awareness.

"I'm just like a TV set, you know? Tuning in to frequency patterns and turning them into meaningful experience?" (Click)

That's it. Oh, you want to hear the technical one? Okay, here it is.

"Intuition resolves the frequency waves of any experience pattern that enters its field, whether from attention or from the universe of patterns directly.

"The meaning we find in these clear pictures from intuition is caused by the varying amplitudes or resonance in the patterns. Amplitude is how far up and down the waves go. The more amplitude, the more the waves resonate in awareness, and so the more meaning awareness experiences from them." (Click)

Next Stop—Attention

Well, this looks like a ball again, but at least this ball moves around. This ball is in orbit around the intuition ball. Goes so fast it looks kind of like the rings of Saturn, you might say.

Just stick awareness in the center, wrap intuition around it, then swing the attention ball around it real fast, and you've got it.

So this here ball is attention. I'll give it a swing, get it going for you. Well, I'd better get it going faster than that. There, that's better. Got it going so fast it makes a blur, don't it? Looks like a ring, don't it?

Ok, I'll push the button now.

"Because intuition tunes in to experience patterns from every direction, it can receive all experience patterns. This is like being aware of the whole universe, all at once.

"If I, attention, don't choose certain patterns, awareness is aware of them all! It's me, attention, that limits experience." (Click)

That's all there is on this one. But there's the technical. I suppose you want to hear that.

"I, attention, am what limits your experience. I tune in to patterns that are in the same plane as my ring. More powerfully resonating patterns register more strongly in me.

"I am a fixed field, and my limit is set. That is, there is only so much of me available. When I tune in to one set of experience patterns, there is less of me available for experiencing other patterns.

"This is what makes it possible for you to be aware of specific experience patterns, instead of being aware of all patterns at once.

"Awareness of personal experience is possible because of me. Without attention, you'd be aware of everything at once...and nothing in particular, not even of yourself as an individual.

"My orbit goes through Beta (material) and Alpha (antimaterial) realities, as well as through universal awareness, so it is possible for me to tune in to any experience pattern. However, I'm usually stuck to the body and mind." (Click)

Yeah, I like that look. I like the looks people get at this exhibit. Blows your mind to find out what makes you who you are, don't it? Yes, yes, here's more technical report.

"We have some control over our attention. This is the only area of consciousness where we have any say at all. We can develop this skill of controlling our attention. Then we can choose what to experience.

"Attention is a two-dimensional field like the rings around Saturn. It encircles intuition. It receives patterns that come in through the outer edge of its ring. These patterns flow through the ring and enter intuition.

"The attention ring reverberates with the resonance of the patterns, so that when the patterns reach intuition, they are stronger than the patterns that come in through other parts of the intuition ball." (Click)

That one always stops kind of sudden.

Next Stop—Mind

Well, we're going to the moons over here. More balls. Ball City, this museum. Just right here is the workhorse called mind. The mind ball and the body ball both orbit around the attention ball. Please watch out for the grease spots on the floor.

"Word patterns are moving through me, mind, as I think. Right now, these exact words are passing through me.

"I can think, but only when attention tunes into me. Otherwise, I'm kind of mindless (ha-ha).

"I can distinguish thoughts by their patterns and arrange them into meaningful new patterns.

"How well I do this depends on how well I have developed myself.

"I've been thinking of changing my name, you know, because people think I am everything—awareness, intuition, attention and mind all in one. I'm good, but not that good." (Click)

Well, we're getting near the end of the tour here. One more ball. Huh? You want to hear the technical. Uh-huh.

"Mind exists as a separate self-aware entity, and was spun off from attention. Mind creates truth. Truth attracts attention and simplifies attention's work.

"Because of its phases through Beta and Alpha, it is an Alpha mind one moment and a Beta mind the next, giving us two minds in one.

"Beta mind was originally limited to resonance with frequencies from the body ball.

"Awareness of the Alpha mind developed later. This changed truth from blind faith in body senses to include a new dimension where antimaterial possibilities could be considered in imagination." (Click)

There's the Theta mind and the Delta mind, too, but that's another tour. This tour here is just the Highlights Tour, guess you know that. You don't understand experience patterns? I don't know if there's any more on that here. Oh well, let's see.

"Experience patterns are made of waves of different amplitudes. These varying amplitudes cause varying amounts of resonance when the patterns pass through awareness.

"We experience this as levels of emotion or meaningfulness or purposefulness or reality.

"The greater this resonance, the more emotional purposeful meaningful reality we experience from the pattern. Resonance is a pure force. Intuition interprets it as meaningful by resonating with its level of amplitude.

"The more resonant experience patterns have larger waves that resonate with awareness. As these pass through awareness, the resonant waves create experience with greater reality, impact and importance.

"While all experience patterns pass through awareness and march into the past, joining a long string of memories, the more resonant experience patterns form a bubble or a bulging frequency wave field on that trail.

"We experience these as our memories, as disconnected segments on the memory trail that have a field of their own from getting puffed up."

That must have been satisfying for you. Here's the one everybody enjoys, body senses. Another ball, of course, also spinning around the attention ball. Watch the floor here, kind of sticky.

Next Stop—Body Senses

"I am so good. When attention is resonating with my patterns, the fields from body senses, awareness forgets everything else and thinks it is in an actual body! Just listen to awareness go on.

"Wow, this is much faster-paced. This is so intense! I can actually feel myself!

"Look at that stuff! I can touch it, I can lift it up. It's easy to make new patterns when they're right there in front of me. I can pick them right up, move them around. This is a trip!

"Oh. Look how they keep changing, some real slowly. Oh oh, some of them are looking ragged. These patterns wear out! They burn out!

"Ugh, this one's heavy. You're telling me that the patterns are heavy here? And that's not all? What else? I have space to contend with? And time? So? What of it?

"I have to move the patterns through space? Those heavy things? And they're constantly losing power?

"My own body too???" (Click)

Well, the ending isn't so great. A little too Twilight Zone for me. Know what I mean? I know, you want to hear the technical.

"Our contact with the three-dimensional physical world is through our body senses. The wave patterns from these senses, such as light and sound frequencies, can be detected by our attention when it is tuned in to the Beta range of 14 to 30 Hz, per brainwave measurement.

"These frequency wave patterns resonate with attention, which then sends them through intuition. Intuition focuses them into experiences for awareness.

"Experience of material or Beta reality, while complex and convincing, is nothing more than experience patterns in a higher frequency waveband.

"While we can help new patterns to manifest physically through direct action in physical reality, Beta reality's laws of time, space and life cycle limit us to temporary creations only." (Click)

Makes life sound like a sand painting on the beach, don't it?

Last Stop—Rest Area

Well, here's the rest area. Gonna drop you off here. Time for me to get ready for the next tour.

You know, they never expect that it's going to be all balls. They think consciousness, oh, that's going to be misty and beautiful rainbows or something, and then it's all balls. Hope you're not disappointed.

Well, anyway, you take care.

Figure One

[NOTE: A Shockwave movie of Sufi George's Dynamic Model of Consciousness can be seen at http://sufigeorge.net/dmc270.swf]

The Dynamic Model of Consciousness is illustrated in an approximate way. The actual substance of the model is frequency wave field patterns.

To fully appreciate the model, it must first of all be visualized in 3-D. That is, the Beta and Alpha loops are best visualized as balloons filled with figure-eight loops that represent experience patterns. These figure-eight loops are of varying sizes and fill the space of the balloons.

These loops are dynamic, that is, each figure-eight loop represents an experience pattern that is traveling its loop path back and forth between Beta and Alpha.

When they pass through awareness from the Beta loop, experience patterns resonate as material realities. When they pass from the Alpha loop, they resonate as antimaterial realities such as thoughts, memories, imaginings and daydreams.

The small center ball is awareness, which is where we experience resonance with patterns as they pass through. A spatial representation is not entirely accurate; it should be visualized as a point without space.

The larger ball represents intuition, and completely surrounds the awareness ball, indicating that experience patterns must pass through intuition which resolves them into condensed, vivid images before they reach awareness. Because its surface points in every direction, intuition can receive experience patterns from any direction.

The ring of attention must be understood as a blur resulting from the rapid orbiting of attention, which is a small ball. The ring of attention has a flat plane, representing its ability to tune in to specific frequency wave patterns, like an antenna.

The depth of the ring, from its outside edge to the inner edge in contact with intuition, provides a focusing effect that condenses the patterns passing through it, making them dominant over intuitive patterns when they reach awareness.

The ball of attention in turn has two "moon" balls orbiting it, representing mind and body. The close proximity of mind and body to attention represents the dominance of their patterns in attention.

The Theta dimension is without boundaries. It is most readily contacted where it joins the Alpha and Beta balloons at the center point in awareness, but with proper configuration of attention, it can be contacted anywhere in the outside universe.

The Beta, Alpha and Theta dimensions meet at the center point of awareness. The Delta dimension is simultaneous awareness of these three dimensions at this center point.

The center crosshairs correspond loosely to the physical brain. The vertical line divides the left and right hemispheres of the brain, and the horizontal line divides the frontal and parietal lobes.

However, this is interesting but not definitive. Remember that the substance of the model is frequency wave fields and not gray matter.

This model represents the typical human condition of being lost or trapped in the patterns radiating from mind and body.

Consciousness as a system consists of awareness, intuition and attention. Of these, only attention is a moving part.

While awareness is typically locked on to patterns delivered by attention, and attention is typically locked on to patterns from mind and body, awareness can be aware of patterns arriving through other points of intuition.

Experience patterns received by awareness can be selected by aware management of attention, or by ignoring attention and focusing awareness on patterns arriving directly through intuition.

Awareness can withdraw into itself so that it experiences only the sense of an aware self, without experience. This experience makes plain the connection of our awareness with the primal awareness of the universe.

Varieties of experience are enabled by configuring the focus of attention in different ways.

The Role of Emotion in Consciousness

Oddly, or so it may seem, emotion does not have a position in the Dynamic Model of Consciousness.

We have seen awareness in the model as a ball, intuition as a larger ball surrounding it, attention as a ball forming a ring around intuition, and little balls for mind and body orbiting around attention.

Where is emotion?

Emotion is a powerful but simple thing. It is the result of resonance, or the power (amplitude) of experience patterns. That is, when the frequency waves of an experience pattern oscillate up and down a lot, they resonate with our awareness more strongly.

Resonance is a wave phenomenon straight out of high school physics. When frequency waves radiate, they trigger radiation in another pattern when certain conditions are met. When the other pattern responds by radiating, this interaction is called resonance.

We can see resonance happening by taking two identical tuning forks, striking one, bringing it close to the other, and listening as the other begins to radiate the same tone (without being struck).

Any pattern with strong amplitude is experienced as meaningful, purposeful, important, and real. This is emotion. Low amplitude patterns are experienced as boring and routine.

It doesn't make any difference whether we call it positive or negative emotion. It's resonance either way.

Emotion is, or can be, a voluntary aspect of our experience. We do not need to be at its mercy. By controlling our attention as patterns pass through it, we can control the degree to which we resonate with the amplitude of the patterns, what we call emotion.

Emotion is nothing more than the amount that attention resonates with the amplitude of experience frequency wave patterns.

Since few of us have developed our skill in actively managing our attention, we just experience emotion rather than manage our experience of it. Without such management, as we all know, we can be victimized by emotion.

With skillful attention management, however, we can choose for ourselves what is important, meaningful, purposeful and real. With the proper skill, we can tune out emotion altogether if we choose. Or we can allow emotion only when we choose. Just because the default mode is to resonate with every amplitude that comes along does not mean that we can't alter our resonance.

We have an attention system that governs our mind, body senses and emotion. But most of us don't center ourselves in our attention.

Rather, we allow our attention to suffer the tyranny of these three as masters, by allowing our attention to be absorbed in them.

Because of such absorption, these three are typically mistaken for "who we are." That's what messes us up. This is the mistake of confusing our experience patterns with our true selves.

We, our true selves, are a consciousness system, consisting of our awareness, our intuition and our attention. We are not our experiences; they're only patterns (frequency wave field interference patterns or morphic fields) that pass through our true selves.

We'll be looking at the way experience patterns repeat. For now, we can acknowledge that they do repeat.

This repetition of experience patterns provides us, each time, with an opportunity to reduce or increase our resonance with the experiences; they're only patterns (frequency wave field interference patterns or morphic fields) that pass through our true selves.

Adjustment is accomplished by management of attention. Put simply, we can either distance our attention from the pattern and let it pass by, thus reducing our resonance, or we can increase our attention to the pattern, increasing resonance.

This will actually adjust the amplitude of the pattern, and when it repeats it will be with decreased or increased resonance.

This is evident from what we already do with our attention, usually without thinking about what we're doing. When we pay a lot of attention to something, to any experience pattern, it becomes more meaningful, purposeful, important and real.

And when we ignore an experience, it loses a degree of these qualities when it repeats in the future.

Attention itself is without emotion. It is capable of resonating with any frequency because it can be tuned, and thus resonates with any amplitude; but in and of itself, it is an emotional blank.

By centering ourselves in our attention system, we can become managers of resonance and cease to be victims of emotion.

We Are Living In Two Universes!

We live in two universes at the same time.

We can call them minds or we can call them universes, because the model of consciousness works just as well as a model of the universe.

We know our brain is divided into right and left sides. We know that the right side deals with the non-symbolic or directly perceived reality, while the left side deals with symbolic and conceptual reality.

We refer to the right side as our material universe, and the left side as our antimaterial universe.

Knowing more, we can call these the Beta mind and the Alpha mind, or Beta awareness and Alpha awareness. We can call them anything, but here's what they really are.

The two minds can be defined by the brain wave frequencies needed to tune into them.

The Beta frequency band, from 14 to 30 Hz (cycles per second), lets us tune into the frequency patterns of three-dimensional "physical" reality, Beta mind reality, body reality.

That is, when our attention is focused on our ordinary day-to-day experience, our brainwaves are in the Beta range. Call this our Beta reality.

When our brainwaves slow down to the Alpha range, 8 to 13 Hz, we are tuned in to another mind.

This mind is also an old friend. We daydream in it, imagine in it, recall our memories in it. When we do these things, our brainwaves measure in the 8 to 13 Hz range.

We usually have both tuned in at the same time, to varying degrees. We can be aware of a car parked at the curb, and at the same time remember one of our favorite cars from the past, for example.

As the frequencies indicate, Beta is a faster world, and we can identify it immediately by the stress of staying tuned into it. Alpha is a slower world, and we experience relaxation and reverie, daydreams and imaginings. The stress is gone.

We can tell which dimension we are the most tuned into by checking our current stress level. Neat, huh? Just like taking a temperature. Feeling high stress? High Beta resonance. Feeling mellow? High Alpha resonance.

In Alpha reality (our antimatter universe), time runs backward, time and space are reversed, matter is antimatter, and things grow weaker instead of stronger.

This sounds simply mind boggling, doesn't it? But we can easily see this for ourselves, and very simply because we live there. Let's just get away from this scientific description for a minute and look at this in terms of things we experience.

Let's deal with time first. We are aware of the future, the present and the past. We see ourselves moving into the future and away from the past. The past is getting older and older in real time, and the future younger.

To our Beta mind, time began in the past with the Big Bang that created the physical universe, and it will march steadily into the future until the Big Crunch. Time flow in Beta is very clearly going into the future.

Suppose instead of moving forward into the future, we just take a seat on the time line and watch our lives pass by? We pick a point, the present, our only choice. And we watch our window of NOW as our experiences pass from the future and into the past.

Only the present is really alive. The future is not alive yet, and the past died. The only time either one is alive is when experience patterns pass through the present.

Our future Beta (material) reality patterns immediately flow out the other side of our window of NOW and become antimaterial memory patterns. We know this; we've never hefted a material memory.

Let's track an experience pattern.

Let's say that in five minutes I'm going to turn on the TV. That experience pattern is in my future. I know it's coming toward me because time is passing.

When the five minutes passes, I turn on the TV as planned. The actual experience is now occurring. That is, the pattern for the experience is passing through NOW, my window of awareness, my seat on the time line.

Immediately, I see it in the past as a memory. After five minutes, I see it as a memory that is five minutes old, five minutes into the past.

Let's check out the memory trail, something we know very well. Or do we?

The trail begins at the window. That's where memories come into being, just at the edge of NOW. It leads into Alpha reality.

We saw this pattern come from the future. We see it moving steadily into the past. The future is Beta reality, the past is Alpha reality.

So you see, time travels backwards in Alpha. Every new second of it is created NOW. The more time flows from the future into NOW, the more the memory is pushed into the past.

In order for us to travel the memory trail (that is, to remember something), we use our Alpha mind. The memories are all connected in a time line, one after the other. The farther along the trail we go, the more in the past we are.

And the past is not time any more. If we want to remember something from ten years ago, we don't have to spend ten years on the memory trail to get to the memory. The memories are just all there now, as if they were in space instead of in time. They are.

We can make a leap in space, but not in time. Jack can jump over a candlestick, in space. But he can't jump into the future or the past.

So the ten-year leap happens in a kind of space, not in time. That is, the only way you can leap is if you have space to do it in.

Memories are neatly arranged in order where we can find them instantly.

Time stops at the window. That strong flow from the future through the present that convinces us that time cannot be stopped, it stops at the window.

This flow of experience patterns from the future, through NOW, and into the past loops around because space is curved.

It curves around into circles in both Beta and Alpha, so that experience patterns travel continuous figure eight loops through our window of NOW. These figure eight loops are our personal universe, with a Beta loop for material reality and an Alpha loop for antimaterial reality.

The same experience patterns flow through Beta, then Alpha, then Beta again, and so on. They are trapped in their figure eight loops. That's why we experience the patterns over and over.

We know our experience patterns do change in time. We watch things grow through life cycles in Beta.

Change is basic, as seen in the fact that our experience is always fresh and new. If we went a day without change, like living yesterday over again, we would experience exactly the same patterns, and we wouldn't have the feeling of change, of new experience.

If our memory patterns continued in time, they would change, the people in them would grow older. But they don't. In Alpha, time is space.

In Alpha space, things grow weaker. We can see this about memories as they fade. In Beta time, things grow stronger. They become more real as they approach NOW.

The time needed to take a leap on the memory trail is always none, essentially, and varies somewhat only because of other activity demanding attention at the moment.

What began as unstoppable time is now spread out before us like space. So we really can see time reversed and time become space.

Time starts with now and heads off into the past. Time is reversed. We can leap through it like it was space, and it doesn't take us any time to do so. Time is space.

If we start with these simple realities that we all experience and can easily understand, and we try to describe them scientifically the way physicists do, we have to say something like, well, in our Alpha universe, matter becomes antimatter, time flows backwards, time becomes space, and things grow weaker.

It sounds awfully difficult and unthinkable, even though it's true.

It's a good thing there's an easy way to see it for ourselves.

Soul?

I do not use the word "soul" in my teaching. It is a prescientific superstition. However, it has been wisely suggested that I write a bridge between "soul" and my teaching, to show the relationships.

If the idea or word "soul" represents something real, then I have some questions about it.

Question: Is it real?
If it is real, can we experience it? Would we know it if we had one? How? And if not, why not?

Question: Is it natural?
If it is real, is it natural? Is it within the natural universe? If it is natural, can it be found? If it is natural, can science find it?

Question: Is it a big deal?
If it's a big deal, well really, wouldn't we know a lot about it from experience? And if it's not a big deal, what is it?

Question: Is it inside or outside?
If it's inside, then where am I? If it's outside, then is it

mine?

Question: If it survives death, what is that?
If there's a permanent aspect of ourselves, is that the soul? Exactly what is it good for? What can it do? What are we talking here?

I used the word "soul" for many years. Now I use the word "awareness."

Awareness is the primary thing, number one. Without awareness, there isn't anything else. If there is no awareness anywhere, there is nothing. The universe goes blank.

Awareness is something very real to me, and if I'm going to have a "soul," I certainly want it to be a real one.

Awareness is the core of who I am. The only happening reality I know about is the reality that passes through my personal awareness.

I cannot define my core self by what I experience; my experience is constantly changing. Rather, I am the one experiencing it. I am awareness, pure and simple.

I am not guilty of my experience. My experience consists of frequency wave patterns that are sometimes managed by me, and that flow through my awareness. The riverbed is not guilty of being wet; it is the water that does that.

My awareness does not need any of the world's religions, for it is not in any difficulty. It is fully operative and healthy.

Furthermore, there is nothing to be done about changing awareness. It is a simple thing, made of the most primitive first cause, and it functions exactly the same everywhere. Only the experience patterns passing through it differ in each case.

Therefore, when I was saved by the scary blood of Jesus, I was saved for nothing. My awareness was not in any danger, nor can it ever be. Awareness is permanent in the universe, the basic unit of the universe.

Is awareness the same as the soul? Hard to say, because no two people can say exactly what the soul is. The soul is a prescientific superstition.

But look at all of the attributes that awareness shares with the general ideas of the soul. And really, if the soul is real, shouldn't it be something obvious to us, not some invisible mystery?

Enlightenment Clearly Explained

The experience of enlightenment is simple to state. It is the experience of awareness only, awareness that is aware of nothing at all except the existence of awareness itself.

During the experience of awareness, the thought-processing mind is empty, body awareness is lost, there is no feeling, and all reality disappears. There is nothing in the imagination, there is nothing anywhere. It is an experience of nothing, of the void.

The key understanding that results from this experience of pure nothing is that one is still alive even when everything is gone. One realizes that one's existence does not depend on anything except awareness itself. One realizes that awareness is the primal reality, the permanent core of ourselves.

The enlightenment experience makes many things immediately clear. It is clear that one's existence does not depend on anything except awareness. This brings complete relief and liberation. It is clear that life is awareness, and not what awareness experiences. So the body, the mind, the physical universe as well as dream universes, feelings, knowledge, are all non-essential to being alive. Fear and guilt vanish because awareness is beyond harm, and experience is not part of one's being.

It is clear that all experience comes from outside of oneself, that experience merely flows through awareness, and that one is not responsible for the helpless act of experiencing one's experience. In short, this state of freedom solves every problem by eliminating it, and provides a completely unburdened peace.

This experience is so attractive, so magnetic, that it cannot be actually forgotten, only displaced by the usual contents and concerns of life. Before the enlightenment experience, one has no idea of life without content. Rather, one's awareness is flooded with content, with all of its concerns and hang-ups.

It should be noted that, after the initial impact of the enlightenment experience wears off, it can be set aside and one can easily slip back into one's old lifestyle patterns. Yet, after the enlightenment experience, one has a yearning for the remembered peace and freedom of the void.

This yearning gradually influences one to decrease the amount of experience in awareness so that there is room in awareness for void. This becomes a balancing act between being aware of void and being aware of experience. The less experience one is aware of, the more void one is aware of, and the freer and more peaceful life becomes.

With too much void and too little experience, however, one becomes an idiot, and so there is the need for learning to balance between void and experience. With enough void in the balance, there is nothing in life that can consume one. Life is fluid and changeable. Life becomes more like a movie than a trap. More accurately, life becomes a group dream.

Yearning for the void influences in the direction of keeping awareness empty of experience. Balancing involves deliberate efforts to remember specific things out of practical necessity. The more experiential content there is in awareness, the less room there is for the void. The more void there is in awareness, the less experience there is, and the less important or consequential experience becomes.

The Stages of Understanding

The model of consciousness is very exciting, and you may want to put it to work for yourself immediately. But. There are stages leading to this point.

The first stage is understanding the components of the model. This is like understanding each component of a stereo system. We need to know what each component is and does before we can see what's happening when they work together as a system.

We will see that awareness simply resonates with experience patterns that flow through it, that intuition simply condenses patterns from everywhere in our universe like a lens, that attention is an antenna that limits access to patterns by its ring design, that body and Beta mind broadcast frequencies that are received the strongest by the attention.

We must understand the logic of the model in the Beta mind, and also understand the scientific description of its reality and how our awareness developed from antimaterial awareness particles or dots.

The next stage is putting the component system together and understanding what it produces as a system—our experience. We will see that patterns flow back and forth between Alpha and Beta realities in figure eight loops, are condensed into vivid reality by intuition, are experienced in awareness, are then expanded back into patterns by the other side of intuition, and are then on their way into Alpha, looping to Beta again.

Then, we need to develop an Alpha understanding of the model by seeing it in action, watching the actual flow of experience patterns through our awareness, and visualizing them flowing through Alpha and back to Beta again.

Then we need to test it for ourselves, creating little test patterns in Alpha and watching them loop through our Beta reality.

Only at this point can we put it to work for ourselves, because we understand and trust it.

There is no way to leap to this point that I know of. However, reaching this point is now a piece of cake compared to the approaches available in the past.

Some work and patience is still required, but it's nothing like the lifetime it took me to get this together. Now, it's down to about 24 to 36 hours of learning and experimentation.

Have that much patience and you'll get it.

Locate Your Crosshair

When an experience pattern passes through awareness, it is at the center of the crosshair part of its figure eight loop. You can sense directly how your Alpha-Beta realities are oriented in yourself, in four steps, by drawing this crosshair.

First, pick a simple experience pattern from your future, something like, when I get back home, I will see the TV set. In what direction did your mind turn to get this pattern? Probably your eyes turned to the right, also.

Next, recall a simple memory from yesterday. For example, yesterday I filled the gas tank. Where was this pattern found? Did your eyes move left also? These two points draw the first line.

Okay, now do a simple arithmetic problem in your head, 22 x 33. Notice where you are doing this. Straight in front in your forehead? That's your Beta mind.

Last, choose a pleasant experience from your past and relive it in your imagination. Where is that happening? In the back of your head? That's your Alpha mind. Draw the crosshair.

The right angle formed by Beta mind straight ahead and the future to the right, Beta reality, describes the direction of your Beta loop or reality.

The right angle formed by the Alpha mind straight behind and the past to the left, Alpha reality, shows the direction of your Alpha loop or reality.

So the bundle of figure eight loops in which your experience patterns travel is oriented at an angle, from behind and to the left, to in front and to the right, or in the quadrants from 12:00 o'clock (straight ahead) to 3:00, and from 6:00 to 9:00.

Get a Peek of Your Alpha Self

Would you like to actually see your Alpha self, in pretty much the same way you see your Beta body? Here's how.

We're going to look at ourselves in a mirror. As we look at the reflection of our Beta self, we will see our Alpha self form over the Beta self and lift off of it, separating itself enough so that we can see it as a separate image.

I just discovered this gateway, and I'll share my experience. I often use a mirror as a device for seeing Alpha patterns as realities, that is, as Beta quality images.

I've experimented with my bathroom wall mirror, with bright lights on and with the lights off. This time, I used a dark bathroom with some daylight coming in.

Now, I'm sure that a lot of what happens here can be explained by various things about our physical eyesight. A negative afterimage, for example, is something the eye creates all the time, and we can see it for about 30 seconds if we close our eyes after staring at something bright for a while. It is actually negative, like a film negative. But that's not what I saw.

Our eyes have a blind spot, and some of the effects I saw can be probably be explained by focusing on the blind spot, like when I saw my entire face go blank.

Two quick points on that. First, this exercise demonstrates that we are experiencing the same patterns in Beta and in Alpha, so of course there will be evidence of seeing with the physical eyes.

Second, explaining how this exercise works misses the point; the point is, here's a gateway for seeing our Alpha pattern vividly, so let's go for it.

I stood in front of the mirror and focused on the reflection of my right eye. At first, I looked at my right eye with my right eye. Later, I focused both eyes on my right eye. There were effects either way, but they changed.

Oh, I also made sure I was standing perfectly straight and relaxing my gut.

I saw my eye in the mirror stand out, separate from the face. The face more or less disappeared. There was a blank area surrounding the eye, and then there was ordinary reflection of the rest of my face and background.

That was one effect, kind of interesting.

Then, several times I saw my face, which is surrounded by hair and so it's like a mask in the mirror. My face got brighter. Then I saw it very clearly as brighter with a flat surface like a photo, with the features prominent but the skin just blank space.

I was focusing on my right eye, and when I saw the face I naturally wanted to look at it, so I moved my focus over to the right and the image blinked away.

So I focused on my right eye some more. I found that I had to look at my right eye constantly if I wanted a stable Alpha image.

So I looked at the changed image of my face, my Alpha face, while keeping my focus fixed on my right eye. And I looked at the face several more times this way.

At this point, I wondered if it was a negative afterimage. I decided to check the eyeball and see if it was dark or light. My eyes are dark, so an afterimage would make them look light. It was dark; all of the features were dark. Positive image.

Now that I stabilized the face, the face became 3-D. The blank skin didn't change, it just wrapped around the shape of my face, and I could see my face like a 3-D mask.

The face looked directly at me. The right eye sparked, changed into something like a vertical opening, dull looking, then went back to normal.

The eyes, eyebrows, nose and mouth all looked like they had been painted perfectly on the mask, and they moved like they were on TV. But the skin looked like plain mask rubber.

These faces lifted away from my Beta reflection, moving closer toward me like about 8 or 10 inches. Also, they drifted around, certainly in part because of my Beta eye movement, but also they were distinctly separate to a small degree.

Two of the faces winked at me. I doubted that it happened the first time, but the second one winked slowly and deliberately. And my Beta eyelids were frozen open all the time.

I asked one face a question, and its eyes looked up to its left as it thought about it. My Beta focus never changed from my right eye.

I then tried to see more, and could vaguely see the shoulders and torso of the face. No big deal, everything important was in the face.

Well, that's it, and I hope you try it.

Now to check it out with the model of consciousness.

Every time I lost the image of the face because I moved my eyes, the reflection of my Beta eye popped back into view. This was a little shock, a very noticeable switch in frequency waves. Then a face eased its way back again, a gradual frequency retuning. Then, whack, lost it again.

My face is a pattern in Alpha and a face in Beta. That is, in Beta, I experience the pattern as material reality, while in Alpha it's an antimaterial pattern.

To varying degrees, I am tuned in to both of these wave bands.

The model says that we just need to focus our attention to certain frequencies and our experience will change. That is, our experience is of the same patterns, but experienced differently.

And that's what happened.

Consciousness Principles from Science

At one time or another, we have all wondered about our own consciousness and the nature of consciousness in general.

In the late twentieth century, our best answers come from our scientists. But because our sciences are each highly specialized, and there is little interdisciplinary communication between them, it's necessary to shop around for partial answers and assemble them into a clear picture.

The present state of affairs in the sciences makes it necessary, for the purpose of understanding consciousness, to find a principle here and a principle there and fit them together in a fresh way.

There is a major division in the sciences today, between those classical (Newtonian) sciences that work only in our objective, three-dimensional reality, and those that work in other dimensions such as subatomic physics.

Most of the pioneers who are exploring consciousness today are stuck because they are trying to discover it by exploring the physical brain, using classical scientific method.

Certainly we are learning some interesting things about the brain this way, and we can use some of the discoveries.

It's the presumption that consciousness is created by the brain that's absurd, yet this is the trap most scientists have fallen into.

Certainly there are relationships between consciousness and our physical brain, but looking for conscious awareness as if it were a product of the brain is a completely backward approach.

Classical scientific method focuses on the study of the objective physical universe, which is why it is investigating the physical brain.

But scientific method never ruled out the use of human consciousness as a variable. Mathematics and consciousness were both accepted as unquestioned fundamentals, although no thought seems to have been given to the acceptance of consciousness as a fundamental until the present century.

Consciousness is such an ever-present condition that it was transparent to early scientists, and they seem to have been unaware that they were accepting it as one of the fundamentals of scientific method. It's a situation similar to that of fish being unaware of the water they live in.

Classical scientists still seem unaware that, in trying to apply scientific method to the discovery of consciousness in the brain, they have entered an area of investigation that is outside the scope of classical scientific method, because consciousness is a presumption of scientific method itself.

Consciousness cannot be studied objectively by classical scientific method because consciousness is itself being used subjectively in the attempt. Consciousness cannot be made a separate, objective thing to study; it cannot be studied without using the thing itself.

We hear from time to time how marvelous it is that the brain is studying the brain. But that's simply not the case. Consciousness is in no way limited to the brain. It's inherent in every subatomic particle in the universe, as we shall see.

Almost all of the progress that scientific method has made in the last three centuries was based on mathematics, with physics having the greatest degree of development.

Classical physics drew the line, though, when it described what it would study. It limited itself to the objective universe, assuming that there was nothing beyond this.

Let me summarize the basic principles of classical physics.

Classical physics is Newton's description of the universe as a machine. All of reality is included in three-dimensional space which is absolute and unchangeable. All changes occur in time. Time is absolute and flows smoothly without regard to anything else.

The universe is made up of material particles, small, solid, indestructible. Gravity is the simple force that acts on particles. All movement is in accordance with mechanical laws, with a cause for every effect. There is a fundamental division between the human observer and the observed universe.

This should sound very familiar to us. This is science as it's been taught to us in school.

During the present century, beginning with Einstein in 1905, every truth of classical physics has been found false. That is, the truths of classical physics have been found to apply only to the objective, three-dimensional universe, and do not apply in the fourth dimension that subatomic physics has discovered.

The first three decades of our century changed the whole situation in physics radically. Two separate developments—that of relativity theory and of atomic physics—shattered all the principal concepts of the Newtonian world view: the notion of absolute space and time, the elementary solid particles, the strictly causal nature of physical phenomena, and the ideal of an objective description of nature. None of these concepts could be extended to the new domains into which physics was now penetrating. [Fritjof Capra, *The Tao of Physics*]

The three-dimensional universe is a lot of territory, but it's not everything, and a scientific truth had been expected to apply to everything.

Modern physics has made discoveries at the subatomic level that defy ALL of the laws of classical physics.

The long search for the basic building block of the universe (it was the atom when I was in high school, although that had already been disproved decades earlier) has led beyond matter altogether.

The universe is no longer seen as a machine, made up of a multitude of objects, but has to be pictured as one indivisible, dynamic whole whose parts are essentially interrelated and can be understood only as patterns of a cosmic process. [Capra]

Classical physics is not dead, but it fails to apply universally, as was taken for granted for such a long time.

This failure created a massive shake-up in the scientific community early in this century. Science as it had been known no longer could be trusted to explain everything.

Today's leading-edge physicists study a non-material universe. That includes our physical universe, now seen as non-material. This is the avenue to understanding consciousness. It's the first scientific proof of the non-material as reality.

So now we can study consciousness as a non-material thing, rather than as a creation of the physical brain. We have proof of the existence of a non-material dimension, from which our physical dimension springs. This is the first principle I am identifying for our discussion.

Personal observation is another important source of information about consciousness. Classical sciences dismiss the importance of personal observation, and this is understandable.

After all, our personal observation tells us that the sun revolves around the earth and that the earth is flat, both of which are no longer true.

But in modern physics, it has been discovered that what the scientist wishes to observe can determine what is observed, and so conscious awareness itself has become a part of the modern scientific process.

Modern physics no longer describes electrons as being material. Today's physicists tell us that particles and waves are two aspects of the same thing; particles are material and waves are non-material. Experiments show that what you look for, whether particles or waves, is what you get.

If we want to see the material universe, we look at particles. If we want to see the non-material universe, we look at waves.

Quantum theory shows us that subatomic "particles" have a tendency (probability) to exist without any certainty of existence in a material way.

In fact, only waves exist until particles are detected by consciousness. Without contact with consciousness, it's all waves and no particles. [Michael Talbot, *The Holographic Universe*]

While we must be cautious about using personal observation, there are nonetheless certain observations that can be trusted if they do not rely on fallible systems such as rational thought process or sensory perception.

Our awareness of our own conscious awareness is the best example of an indisputable personal observation about consciousness.

This observation lacks consensus, since we can only be aware, usually, of our own conscious awareness and not that of another person. However, consensus would be a lesser proof, satisfying the thought-processing mind only with nothing more than statistics, and the mind is not needed to make the personal observation in the first place.

Without hearing it from scientists, everyone already knows directly that consciousness is not a physical thing, because everyone has conscious awareness and can check it out first-hand. It can be experienced immediately and directly.

Understanding consciousness, though, is a matter of satisfying the thought-processing rational mind, and to do that we need a theoretical explanation with a solid foundation.

Knowing that non-material things exist, that the "basic building block" of the universe is so many non-material patterns, that everything physical is made of something non-material, gives us rational confidence in approaching consciousness as a non-material thing.

With that confidence, we can take advantage of the singular fact that consciousness is the one thing that can be studied directly, since every one of us is right in the middle of it, and everything else is outside of it.

Since consciousness is a real non-material thing and is immediately accessible by everyone, why not study it first-hand? Doesn't this make a lot more sense than looking for clues in the physical brain? Why settle only for clues about something that we already have right in front of us?

Can anyone deny the reality that we have awareness, that we are aware? Some modern physicists finally accept this as an integral aspect of scientific inquiry. In fact, they acknowledge that there can be no scientific inquiry without this awareness, and that the results of scientific inquiry are in part actually determined by awareness.

This scientific conclusion is already some 50 years old, yet it has not penetrated our pool of common sense knowledge. Within the sciences, however, it has made possible some additional work that has great importance to a study of consciousness.

Morphic field theory, a major contribution by Rupert Sheldrake, establishes a non-material field for every physical reality, a field that exchanges information with its physical counterpart.

In psychophysiology, Stephen LaBerge established the reality of the dream state, the first non-material dimension of reality acknowledged by science as one that can be directly experienced. His experiments also established the reality of being consciously aware in two dimensions at the same time, which so far has been little appreciated for its remarkable implications.

These landmark discoveries, taken together in an interdisciplinary manner, provide a foundation for making consciousness understandable.

In addition, today's common knowledge includes an understanding of nested systems theory, the idea that a big thing is made up of lots of little things, which are made up of lots of even littler things. The structure of nested systems is invaluable in understanding the structure of consciousness.

Consciousness itself is a thing. According to modern physics, the idea that there are material things in the universe is outdated. Every thing is fundamentally a non-material pattern.

This description applies especially well to consciousness. We can say that consciousness is a pattern, just like any and every other thing or reality.

From there, we can observe some of the attributes and behaviors of this complex pattern.

Mind is usually the first thing that "comes to mind" when we talk about consciousness. Descartes thought that because he was able to use his mind, this proved his existence. He completely overlooked the fact that the thought process can be halted, and that it is awareness itself that undeniably self-proves existence.

Is mind the same as consciousness? No. Mind is a tool, and it is not even necessary to conscious awareness. Mind is a thought-processor, and we do not need to think thoughts to exist (although, in our three-dimensional reality, it does help). If my mind goes blank, I still exist, don't I?

Consciousness has awareness as its primary attribute. Consciousness is a thing, patterns. Awareness is what most people mean when they say consciousness, but let's be more careful about the words we use here.

Awareness is the attribute of consciousness that experiences patterns after they are focused by intuition.

Intuition, in turn, has attention as one of its major attributes. Attention, perhaps, is the aspect of greatest personal interest because it is what gives us an identity as a separate being, by restricting our experience to certain patterns.

One way we use attention is to think thoughts, to use the mind. Mind processes thoughts. It's just a tool of attention.

We can use it, or we can turn it off.

Many of us use our minds so constantly that we identify with them. Like Descartes, we make the mistake of assuming that thinking is the same as being aware.

For many, the idea of stopping our thoughts seems impossible. But it is possible to stop the thought process. We can know this from personal experience, as is attested to by many who practice deep meditation, people who use mind machines, etc.

We all space out from time to time. There are no thoughts passing through our awareness at such times. There is no language. There is no use of mind.

We can categorize mind as an optional process, and need not confuse it with awareness itself.

Awareness is the primary process of consciousness. We can stop being aware of our thoughts and set the mind aside, but we cannot set awareness itself aside.

We are always aware, even when we are aware of nothing in particular, or are aware only of awareness itself.

Descartes would have been correct saying, "I am aware, therefore I exist."

Awareness is the only remaining mystery of the universe. Once we accept awareness as a reality, awareness itself explains everything else.

Patterns themselves conceivably might not require awareness to exist, though they have it. By themselves, they would exist as possibilities which conceivably could never progress beyond that stage. A possibility without awareness to experience it is a very remote kind of reality, indeed.

We're going to accept awareness as our primary reality. None of us has any question about doing so. It is an immediate and direct knowledge that we don't have to think about and which certainly does not depend on any of our physical senses. Rationally, it is the winning qualifier for a non-material reality, since it is the most directly real non-material thing we know.

Awareness is our starting point in understanding consciousness. Again, consciousness is a thing, a pattern, the kind of basic reality described by modern physics, and it has awareness as its primary attribute.

How do we know that these patterns have awareness? We are starting out, of course, with undeniable knowledge that awareness is a fact of the universe. But there is scientific support, too.

Bell's Theorem provides some confirmation that the patterns making up the universe have awareness. Briefly, the theorem describes a curiosity regarding the opposite spin of paired electrons.

If the spin of one electron is measured on a horizontal axis, the other instantly spins in the reverse direction on a horizontal axis, even if it is located galaxies away, well beyond the limit of the speed of light, and even if it was previously spinning on a vertical axis.

The experimenter can determine whether the electron he is investigating spins horizontally or vertically. The phenomenon of interest is that the paired electron is somehow aware of what the experimenter has done, and it assumes a spin on the same plane, vertical or horizontal, and it does so instantly.

We know that in the three-dimensional universe nothing travels faster than the speed of light. This communication behavior of electrons is explainable only by a characteristic of the fourth dimensional world of subatomic physics.

Only awareness can account for this immediate communication between the pair of electrons.

We know that awareness exists, first-hand. We can observe readily that awareness operates instantly, that there is no time-based process involved. This is what we are referring to when we describe an intuitive "flash," for example.

Bell's Theorem shows us that even electrons exhibit awareness. No other known explanation is fast enough to account for the phenomenon.

Within our three-dimensional reality, classical science still works, and we have all long been familiar with the nested systems theory of electrons forming atoms, atoms forming molecules, molecules forming elements and so on.

We now understand that this process begins farther back, with the non-material, and ends in the apparent material.

So, we arrive at the broadened principle that the universe is a single entity that is non-material and aware, and which contains the physical universe as a non-material specialization of patterns.

By combining nested systems theory with morphic field theory, we can see the universe as a morphic field made up of lesser systems of morphic fields.

Rupert Sheldrake in *The Presence of the Past* observed that a certain kind of bird learned to take the paper cap off of milk bottles on the doorstep and drink some milk.

The puzzle he confronted was that this same kind of bird in distant locations also learned the same trick, yet the birds had no physical way of communicating.

He developed the theory of morphic fields to explain the phenomenon. A morphic field is a non-material "energy" field that contains the information patterns (of consciousness) for a given physical reality.

Morphic fields have a strong tendency to mirror their physical counterparts in terms of patterns of information. This awareness of information exists as a loop between the morphic field and the physical counterpart, which is how the distant birds learned the bottle cap trick.

This theory also agrees with critical mass theory, as in the story of the hundredth monkey, which, when in his turn was trained to do a certain task, tipped the community scale so that all of the non-trained monkeys suddenly could do it, too.

Sheldrake restricted his discussion of morphic field theory to biology, and his work is a major contribution to the refinement of evolutionary theory.

I have shifted from his emphasis on the biological, from the three-dimensional physical world, and focused on the non-material morphic field itself. This gives us ground for subdividing conscious awareness into various levels of morphic field systems.

As a thing, as with any thing, a morphic field is made of patterns that have awareness. Sheldrake has identified several specific morphic fields, for example, the morphic field that contains the aware patterns for a community of birds.

Within that community morphic field, the morphic field for each bird is a separate sub-system. The community morphic field is made up of all of the individual morphic fields of each bird.

Systems theory is characterized by the expression, "the whole is greater than the sum of its parts." That is, a larger system is a somehow greater kind of entity than the mere total of its sub-systems.

An easy example is the human body. Each organ is a sub-system, yet the whole, the human body, is a greater kind of entity than the mere total of its organic systems.

Since we can accept the existence of non-material realities, our own awareness for example, we can accept the reality of morphic fields. The morphic field has been demonstrated by Sheldrake sufficiently to be acceptable as a scientific reality, although this theory is currently held in disrepute because of the difficulty of proving or disproving it.

Our consciousness, with its awareness, is a morphic field. Some of its aspects are reflected in the physical counterpart of the brain, but the whole being greater than its parts, the brain does not reflect all of consciousness.

We have, then, the principle that conscious awareness exists in reality as a morphic field, and is composed of nested systems of morphic fields.

Actual personal experiences of other dimensions of reality, which is as yet beyond the reach of the same physics that discovered them, has been scientifically established by psychophysiology.

The phenomenon of interest here is the lucid dream. A lucid dream is a dream in which the dreamer is asleep and dreaming, yet awakens into a state of ordinary awareness in the dream and is fully aware that he is in the dream reality.

This phenomenon was long dismissed by scientists as an impossible delusion until Stephen LaBerge proved its reality [*Lucid Dreaming*]. He wired dreamers to electronic equipment to prove they were in stages of sleep, and recorded the eye movements that occur during dreams, called rapid eye movements or REM.

Lucid dreamers communicated from the dream state with pre-arranged eye signals that were recorded electronically, proving that the lucid dream experience, experience of another dimension within ordinary conscious awareness, was in fact very real.

So we have the principle that other dimensions of reality can be experienced in waking conscious awareness.

These, then, are the principles I have assembled from various sciences and used to lay the foundation for our understanding of consciousness.

The Categories of Things

The first order of things has only one thing in it, and that is the first thing, awareness.

The second order of things is frequency waves and their patterns, interactions, interferences, and other behaviors.

The third order of things includes the four wavebands on which we can experience reality.

The fourth order of things includes the space available to our attention when it is not primarily focused on an experience waveband.

First Order Thing

The first thing is awareness. Until there is awareness, there is nothing else. There can be nothing else.

Awareness is the first thing in the universe. We are aware. We have the same thing that was there before the beginning of the universe.

Awareness was there before there was any kind of reality, whether material (Beta), imaginary (Alpha), dream (Theta), or lucid dream (Delta).

This means, if all of our reality disappeared, we would still be there with our awareness.

Our awareness is, therefore, the permanent part of ourselves.

We have always been aware, and we will always be aware. What we are aware of changes, but that's something different from awareness itself. That's experience.

Second Order Things

Frequency waves and the patterns they form are the second order of things.

Frequency waves, our scientists tell us, are as basic as you can get when you look for the basic building blocks of the universe. Beyond material particles are the antimaterial frequency waves, also call strings, that give material its shape and substance. Material reality is all an illusion, in a way.

Every reality we can comprehend in any way is made of frequency waves. Frequency waves are the stuff that everything is made of. This conflicts with our common knowledge, because science has advanced much faster than our common sense.

Third Order Things

The four wavebands on which we experience reality are like a multiplex theater that we're born with.

When we wake up in the morning, we check in to the Beta Theatre, our ordinary daily reality.

And then we go to bed. In bed, we begin to fall asleep from Beta and wake up in the Alpha Theater, land of imagination, reverie, daydream, memory. It's an antimaterial world, and it's completely private and personal. Anything at all is possible there, and it's all perfectly safe.

Then we fall asleep from Alpha and wake up in the Theta Theater, the land of our common dreams. This is another antimaterial world, a world that disappears when it's no longer needed, but what a theater!

In Theta, everything seems real. Of course, our Theta mind is thick-headed, almost stupid, compared to our Beta mind, but we don't realize this, usually, until we think about it in Beta.

So we'll believe anything in Theta. What a convincing interactive 3-D experience!

When we're fortunate, we wake up in the Delta Theater, perhaps suddenly seeing our Theta scene roll over into this land of living life, this ultimate reality trip.

Delta is the lucid dream state, more real than Beta, tremendously exciting, full of fascinating and rewarding possibilities!

The Fourth Order

The fourth order of things is found in the space between the four wavebands of experience. In this space, experience patterns fade out and the void fades in.

That is, our attention moves from the experience patterns in the wavebands to the space between them. It's what we pay attention to that's changing here.

Fourth order things include the variety of experience patterns before they fade completely after starting at the beginning.

Then, at the end, the order includes the state of pure awareness, awareness itself, awareness not aware of anything else at all except of itself, of its awareness.

It's been called enlightenment, samadhi, satori, salvation, illumination, but I'm telling you what it really is, generically. My explanation is the skeleton of almost every other explanation. It's withdrawing our attention to that space. And I call it enlightenment.

About Patterns

The Dynamic Model of Consciousness is a pattern of consciousness.

A pattern is invisible. It is something we can imagine, but imagining a pattern is not the same as seeing it. To imagine a pattern we need to give it some kind of image or sound, or something to put up there on our Alpha Screen of imagination.

To see a pattern, then, we have to dress it somehow, like putting clothing on an invisible man. Once the clothing is on, we can see the man's pattern clearly.

It is the elements of the earth that come together in the pattern of a rose bud; the hungry who come together into the pattern of a restaurant clientele. Indeed, the elements of our own physical bodies give our personal patterns a reality in Beta, our usual material world.

The patterns are there first. They have to be, or the particles have no idea how to move. Movement presupposes patterns to move through, even if that pattern is simply a straight line. We don't move our bodies without thinking about where we want to move them. If it were random, just imagine our seizures. We follow patterns: to the right or left, or whatever.

In the universe, patterns are a primordial reality, an early level of manifestation. It doesn't take much to create a pattern, since it's not made of anything. What a pattern is made of is like seeing what the invisible man would look like naked. It can be seen by imagining it with clothing.

The way we know the patterns are there is because we know what they look like when we clothe them with frequency waves. As waves, we can see patterns clearly.

Waves are easy to visualize. They ought to be, since they are the recognized "basic building blocks" of the universe. They are the first pattern in the universe. One way and then the other, and then back again.

The Dynamic Model of Consciousness is made of patterns that are visible when waves pass through. The DMC itself is made of patterns. As such, it is a real thing, since patterns are real things.

The patterns in the DMC include the way intuition focuses frequency waves so we can see them, and the way attention selects our experiences by tuning in to frequency waves.

You can see for yourself how these patterns work together to enable you to be aware of experience. Visualize them as frequency waves. Put clothes on them. Then you can see each pattern working, and you can see how well the clothes fit the reality you know as yourself.

Conversely, when you are looking only at the clothes, you may not see the pattern at all.

Orbits, the First Pattern

The first pattern in the universe is the orbit. The orbit is the first instance of a frequency wave doing something more than simply sitting somewhere as an isolated dot of awareness.

The orbit is an illusion, of course, and can be seen in various ways.

A very slow moving orbit appears as the ball that is in orbit. Our best example of a ball in orbit that can only be seen as a ball is the ball Earth. We see it as a stopped ball because our perspective of Earth is in synch with the speed of Earth's orbital travel. Our astronauts report being awed at seeing Earth from a different perspective.

A fast moving orbit appears as a circle. We've all seen a ball on a string being swung around in a circle. Done fast enough, we see a circle there in the air, where there is no circle really. The pattern of the circle is there, and can be seen when frequency waves, such as the swinging ball, pass through it.

A very fast moving orbit appears to us as solid, as made of matter. However, if our perspective were on the ball in a very fast moving orbit, it would appear to us as a stopped ball, because we would be going very fast also. Matter as we normally see it is an illusion created by very fast frequency waves.

The orbit is the first true pattern in the universe. Everything else comes from the balls that several orbits combine to produce, which become particles of atoms, which become molecules, which become elements, which become matter. But it's orbits all the way, combining themselves into increasingly complex patterns.

So exactly what is an orbit? It is a circle pattern that is made of nothing at all. There is a particle in it, and there is the circle pattern that the particle is following, but the only way it can be seen as an orbit is from a perspective that lets us see the particle traveling very fast in its orbit.

This is easy to do, as with the ball on a string. What's not so easy to do is to realize that all balls are in orbit, especially when we see them as not moving at all.

When we take into account our rotation pattern on Earth, what we get is a pattern of ourselves corkscrewing our way along the orbit of Earth. This corkscrew pattern gives us a base up-and-down pattern to our lives, and it is of fundamental importance because we can influence it.

What we experience as ups and downs in our lives and as going in circles, reflects the two basic patterns of life, which combine into the corkscrew wave. The corkscrew wave is what gives us the opportunity to go up when we are going up, and go down when we are going down.

The point is, when we are going up and we know it, we can go up higher. And when we are going lower, we can put on the brakes. This will pull us out of the corkscrew pattern and into our chosen pattern.

The corkscrew pattern is nature's way of saying, if you're just going to sit down through life, here's your basic minimums. The screw keeps passing through you, lifting you up and dropping you down. You ride it like a carousel (up-and-down + orbit patterns of a carousel = satellite pattern).

The Amazing Life of an Antimaterial Dot

In the model of consciousness, awareness itself is the starting point because it is our only unassailable truth and our most fundamental reality. In the theory behind the model, awareness is the primal reality of the universe and, given its existence, is the only remaining unexplained mystery of the universe.

The intuitive truth of our awareness is not something science can ever disprove.

Rather, science would be impossible without awareness and has assumed it all along, although not explicitly until recent decades.

Therefore, a model of consciousness must assume the presence of awareness as its starting point.

This story portrays the development of a primal antimaterial awareness particle or "dot" to its maturity as a consciousness system that's about to become aware of matter. It shows what the particle could possibly be aware of at each stage, given its experience.

I am an antimaterial dot floating in space, in nothingness.

And this is My Life.

I am aware of my awareness.

I'm aware of myself as a dot.

And that's about it.

I guess I'm just stuck.

All I can see is myself. There's really nowhere to look. There's no up or down, there's no sideways, nothing.

I have a very boring existence.

I don't even have any size. There is no space to have size in here, anyway. There's only me, my awareness. And I'm just a point. No part of me sticks out in any direction.

And just look at time here. There isn't any.

I am aware of the present instant, as far as time goes. There is no actual time. It's just now, always now.

If I try to look at my past, it looks exactly the same as my present because nothing ever changes. I just continue on as a dot now.

If I try to look at my future, it looks the same, too. It's more awareness of now. So I don't understand time, because nothing changes here. Really, there's no such thing as time. It's just always now.

If something would only change, then I could have time, a past, present and future, instead of just the present.

If something would happen, and I mean anything at all, then I could have a second experience, something to experience besides myself.

Afterward, I could say, oh, this happened before, and I would have something in the past to relate to. And then I could wonder about something happening again, and I would have a future.

But no, I don't have these things, and so I don't have time. Just now, always now.

Something Happens!

Finally, something happened! It was really exciting!

It was really something! Suddenly, I realized that I am not alone in the universe!

There is someone else! And you know what that did to me? It changed me!

It literally changed me from a dot to a line! I'm a line now! Actually, we are a line, since it takes both of us to make the line. What do you think, how do we look? Can you see us? We have a dimension! And it goes from here to there, from me to...him. He's so magnificent. He looks just like me, you know.

I found out he's another dot, like me. He bumped into me, really interfered with me. I didn't know dots moved. Well, I didn't even know there were other dots, so what do I know? I suppose with your fancy Alpha-Beta mind, you see us as just another standing frequency wave, don't think I don't know that. But you saw where I grew up, and I think I've done okay, becoming a line.

We take walks now. They're not very long, but we really enjoy them. We can move from one end of our self to the other.

The walk is ever so much better than being a dot because together we are a one-dimensional being.

When we're alone, just dots, he's just like me, a good-for-nothing. But you know, when we get together, we share a kind of vision.

We see together that there is a here and a there, my awareness and his awareness, and it feels like there is space where we can either be separated or united. Space is so exciting!

And we are aware that sometimes, or maybe at the same time, it's hard to tell, we can be just single dots. It's happened before and it'll happen again. So it seems like there's time in our vision, a past when we were dots, and a present when we are a line.

Maybe it's just reference points in relation to ourselves, but it feels like time, do you know what I mean? Well, it may not mean much to you, but even having a glimmer about time is really great for us.

So a lot has changed since I was just a little dot. We walk back and forth a lot together, enjoying our vision. It's a nice life. For a change!

Something Else Happens!

Since you last wrote about us, it seems like a million years ago, a truly amazing thing is happening. It leaves me almost speechless!

We have a terrible accident, but it turns out to be for the best. We are side-swiped by another line!

It smacks right into the middle of our line, a direct 90-degree hit. And it stays there! It won't go away. But that's for the best, as I'll tell you.

Now, we've got this big dent in our middle, and when we walk we have to walk the curve to the right, or to the left, depending which way we're walking. But you know, once we got used to it, it became our curve and it gives us some variation in our exercise.

The neat thing about the curve is that it lets us move in space in new directions, to the right and to the left again. So now we have two dimensions to walk in, back and forth, and side to side.

We saw that right away by walking the curve. Now we know about sideways, a different space from the one we had before.

It's very neat, but it's not as big a deal to us as it was getting the first dimension.

Real interesting, but not the same thrill.

We are troubled about there being other lines out there. If there are, they could change us even more. We wonder how.

We have to figure that if there are other lines, then there are other spaces in those lines.

And we also have to figure that lines are moving, since one hit us. And that some lines get dented when they are interfered this way. And that another accident is likely at any time.

If we have more accidents, we don't know what it will lead to.

The new space we walk into when we walk the curve is from the other line, since it's going the other way. We had to get acquainted with the other line before we could walk the curve, so now, really, there are four of us united when we walk.

What is mind-boggling is what more of these accidents might do to our time.

We could have three reference points: ourselves as dots, ourselves as a line, and ourselves as two lines, and who knows what might come next? The dots were first, the line was second, and other lines would come third.

These events would be in our past as memories. When we put them in order, they would make a past, our own real past with real events to remember.

We would have both a real present and a real past! We'd have real time! Well, you say it only moves one way. But we say, yaa-hoo!

And Something Else! No Kidding!

A lot has happened. First, since we now have a past of our very own, let us tell you about what you missed.

Once upon a time, there was a dot. Oh, having a past feels so good! Well, enough of that.

First, we got acquainted with the other line. There were two dots in the line, just like us. We found out that the other line had been just like us, living in their own space, and then they met.

When we became aware of the other line's space, it became aware of our space, and together we four gained a second dimension for ourselves. We needed each other so we could all experience two dimensions.

Really, we had to become all one together. It took some adjustment, but we have it now and we see both lines at the same time, one going this way and one that, making a two-dimensional space.

We've more or less stopped thinking about ourselves as dots now. We are so comfortable together (we are all exactly alike) and we enjoy our experience when we're together.

The fact is, our space goes out all around us now. It looks like a big, well, flat space. When we walk forward, we can sense space on both sides.

We have to look for this space, and it's hard to see because there's nothing in it. We can't really see it, but we understand that it's there. When we walk, we know that we are walking somewhere on this space.

We're hoping that other lines will hit us and fill up some of this space. Isn't that a change from being afraid of other lines? The only place we can go for a walk now is back and forth and sideways around the curve.

If we get some other lines involved, we'll have new places to walk. We'll be able to walk sideways at any point, and back and forth at any point. Isn't that nice to think about?

Oh, No! Another Something!

Great news! We've gone into the land development business!

It happened just as we hoped. Lots of other lines hit us and what we pictured actually happened—we now have a gorgeous field. We walk everywhere, all together as one. We are very big, so many dots all united.

And that's not all. You'll never guess what else.

Some lines interfered with our field by hitting us from below and going right through us to above. We'd never thought about below and above before. Can you imagine it? We have three dimensions now! Isn't that great news?

We have hills! And valleys! There are lots of places where we can jump from one hill to another. We can move in any direction we want, now. We all get together in one united dot, and we walk back and forth, side to side, up hills and down hills.

When I think back to the time when I had no space at all, I am simply overwhelmed at the changes that have happened over the past few million years. We all are, since we have to be all one to realize our three dimensions.

Now we have land! Real land that goes in all directions. I mean, we go roaming and exploring everywhere. And it keeps on growing. There's no end to it!

You know what else? We have a future, a real one, not just an idea about it. We've paid attention and noticed that there is a pattern to the way the lines hit us. Sometimes there's a lot at once, and other times are quiet. There's something regular about their arrival.

We know when to expect the interferences! Lots of them are evenly spaced, so we know when, in the future, they are coming. We have a future that we know something about! We can predict our experiences!

Our life has become very complicated compared to our existence as mere dots. We can experience three dimensions in space, something we didn't even know about originally, and we have three kinds of time, also something we never suspected. Past, present and future.

Can you imagine how this changes our experience?

Our new life is really grand. We spend all of our time all together as one so we can experience our land in 3-D and watch it grow in time.

We are feeling like a king these days. We have a domain. Why, we are a domain!

What? Even Something More Happens?

Eventually, we noticed a strange thing happening to us. As we grew more and more, our land began to dip downward.

We didn't know what to think, at first. We worried about it. And it kept happening.

Our lines were getting longer and that was fine because it gave us longer walks. But we couldn't see over the horizon any more, and we felt queasy, heading for what looked like empty space.

Eventually, our land dipped so far and so much that it connected itself into a sphere.

Now, our land is a big ball, and that's real different for us. We have an actual shape now.

You know what this did? Instead of line paths going this way and that and up and down, each dot's path was connected to its own tail. It created circle paths for our dots. Now our dots just go around and around, side-by-side. We love it!

There are two places on our ball where our paths all cross over. One is on top of the ball, and one at the bottom. We had to stagger our walks so we could all cross those points without colliding with each other.

What happened then is pretty amazing, too. While we experience our dots just walking along every place else on the ball, at the two crossover points we experience this huge rush of dots.

It is dazzling to see. We are going by these two points in such rapid succession that we all just blur into a kind of glow. We feel tremendously united at these two points, really concentrated.

So now we have these two glow points as curiosities.

Our lines have their own curiosities, too, now that they are also circles.

Really, our lines have all turned into circles! Big circles. And you should see the traffic! We have to cross over everybody else's path, and we mean everybody's. I mean, we felt united before, but the feeling of unity is really powerful at these two points.

We had to adjust to this change into a ball. Basically, all we did was situate our dots so none of them was exactly next to each other. That way, when we passed the points, we missed each other, just by a hair, of course, but we avoided crashing into each other.

Everything is just humming along now.

Our circles are happy, too, as you see. Still think of themselves as lines sometimes, even as dots, but they're getting used to being circles. And of course, we all think we are a ball when we pass the two crossover points.

Something Happens...Revisited

Hello, again! Lots of news to share.

Now we have two places to enjoy our combined awareness to the max. At these points, we are really powerful. We understand everything about our ball, every dot in it. It is so magnetic at those two points that the crossover experience stands out as our most impressive and important experience.

However, it is changing us.

It seems that since we have been paying the most attention to our dots when we pass the two points, we are less aware of ourselves as dots when we are elsewhere in our circles.

In fact, just about all we think about is looking forward to reaching the crossover points.

What's changing is this. Our circles are becoming weak around the middle from lack of attention.

We're upset about this because now when our dots walk, we are not exactly circles any more. Our ball is starting to flatten out around the middle, getting a waist, because all we think about is the crossover points.

The problem is that the shape of our ball is changing. We're worried; what might we turn into? A cucumber? It's frightening to think about.

We all know this change is happening, but none of us really wants to do anything about it. If we pay more attention to our ball's waist, then we won't enjoy the crossover points as much. Nobody is willing to give up that pleasure.

Again! Something New Happens!

Our news is really incredible this time.

We are just so glad that it's finally over. Our waist kept shrinking and shrinking until it was just a point. It changes us so that, now, really, we are two balls, connected by a point in the middle.

We are completely different! Who could have expected this to happen?

Our dot walk has really changed. When we get to the new point between the two balls, we just keep on going and we're in the other ball. And it's a straight shot at the crossover, so we can't miss.

Our path just keeps on going around the other ball until it gets to the center point again, and then it switches to the first ball, like a figure eight.

We still have our two glowing spots of combined awareness, but now they are on two different balls!

Here's the major news. At the new meeting place, where the balls connect in the middle of our figure eight path, our dots end up, on one figure-eight walk, crossing the point twice. You know what that means?

Traffic jam! We have to get through the point twice as fast or else we'll bump into each other. So we had a big lesson to learn at the moment when our waist became a point and we started crossing paths there.

You should have seen the collisions at first! Talk about fireworks! But we figured out that we could go through the point twice as fast by passing each other side by side.

One goes one way, one the other, at right angles.

The way it works out wasn't totally great at first, because when half of us are on one ball, the other half is on the other ball. It taxed us somewhat to divide our awareness between them. It made us into, like, two separate awarenesses, even though we are really still all one. This was a difficult adjustment for us to make, believe me.

But once we got past that, we found a great new thing. We now have a third glow spot at our new center point, and it's twice as bright as the other two, and that's a huge surprise! We are finding that this third glow spot is the easiest one for being aware of all of ourselves. It gives us a way of letting us see our two balls as two parts of one us.

And it means that we can be aware of all of our self as one awareness.

Before, we never even thought about how we were divided in two when we were just a ball, since only half of us were at one of our two crossover points at any given time.

There's something interesting going on at the three points. We can feel it when we pass through them.

It's like at the two original glow points, each one is doing something different. It's like each one is a separate mind. And in the new, brighter glow point in the center, everything is combined together, and it's a real power place to pass through, like a kind of super mind.

We are feeling rather complete these days. We have two minds where we can watch our dots, when they are on one ball and when they are on the other, separately. And we have a special place where we can see them together, at our center point.

We are feeling rich with perspectives!

The Last Something Else!

Our rocking chair days, yes! This is really getting kicked back. Rocking and thinking, looking back on my long life.

I look back and remember things, you know? Just think about them. All those great moments.

I remember when I was just a dot, just a single cell, so to speak. Then growing up and becoming a line, and then a circle. How surprised and pleased I was with myself!

Being a ball was the first really major challenge of my life. Being a ball is complicated, you know, what with those two hot spots on them.

But after many eons, I got adjusted, then bored. In my boredom, I decided to see if I could find anything different about my two centers. I mean, I knew that they were exactly the same. The same dots crossing the same points, just again.

It was a game I made up, trying to find differences between the two centers which were the same as each other.

In all the time I played that game, the only difference I ever found was that if I am in one center, the other center is opposite, the one I'm not in. Thought that was pretty useless information, at the time.

But then I noticed that in one center I saw north was up. And in the other center, north was up, too. But in one center, I was experiencing north directly and only remembering the north of the other ball.

That was a difference. One north was real now and the other was a memory. Of course, that switched around when I moved to the other center.

Since it was a difference, I decided to call the remembered center south. It was hard to keep them straight at first; I had to keep track of where I was.

Then I noticed that the ball is spinning. When I was at the north center, the ball spun clockwise. That meant that, even though it was part of the same ball spinning the same way, from my perspective at the north center I had to consider the south center as spinning counterclockwise.

That is, in the north center, if I look up, the spin is clockwise. The same spin in the south center is counterclockwise when I look up because I'm looking in the opposite direction.

So I was finding more and more opposite things about the north and south centers. It was located in an opposite direction, it was spinning in an opposite direction, and when one was a real experience the other was just a memory.

This all became much easier to understand after I changed into a figure eight. With two separate balls, it's much easier to keep them straight in relation to each other.

Before I became a figure eight, I used to just torture myself wondering about that contrary oppositeness. But now it's much easier to understand.

Let's just pick one ball and say that's where I hung out mostly. So we're there, right?

Take a look around. All of this land is mine.

The other ball is in my memory, in my past. Opposite. It's in my past—I'm not experiencing it, I'm remembering it, I'm just tuned in to my one ball, here. Pay attention.

I have been in the other ball, right? Right now, limiting my awareness to this ball, I am therefore not aware of the other ball as a real experience. All I have here is my memory of it. (I never deal with anything I can't be aware of.)

So from here, the other ball has my land as my past memories of it. From here, my land in this ball and my memories of my land in the other ball are in two different times. My land is here where it's going to stay, and my memory in the other ball is headed off into the past as memory.

In this ball I see my land surviving into the future, experience it surviving moment by moment. I can feel time marching on, carrying me with it.

As for the other ball, I can only remember this time on my memory trail, and it's there in the order I paid attention to my land, you know, looking here, looking there.

All of these lookings at my land that I experience in my time become my memories, right? And these memories are in the other ball.

My memory trail is steadily moving into the past. My experience is always shoving each memory farther into the past.

So as my real land moves into the other ball, from my experience to my memory on the figure eight trail, it becomes time, my past. Time. And it's running backwards, opposite.

There was one more thing. As my experiences became memories, they stopped being real land and became just memories of land. They went from matter to antimatter, just like that. Opposite.

So now, here I am, half this and half that, half real and half memory, half material and half antimaterial, a real split personality.

Yet, when I center myself at my center crossover point, it all makes sense as one me.

That's where I spend my time now, mostly, at my center point. It's just no good being split in two.

Back when I was just a dot, I was just me. Now, after all I've been through, I'm just me once again. Funny how things work out.

Of course, I'm a much more sophisticated me, now. Been thinking of giving myself a sophisticated name. "Electron" keeps running through my mind. What's your opinion? Good name?

Carrier Waves
Illustrating the FEAR "Typical Response Pattern"

The prospect of change is faced with a variety of responses among different people. When faced with an opportunity for change, some may react with fear, others with interest, and others with something else.

Why do different people have different responses to change? This can be answered by looking at how they acquired the responses they are using.

In order to experience a "typical response" pattern like these, that pattern must exist in one's collection of experience patterns. That is, one must have experienced it before.

When an experience pattern enters our consciousness system from outside of our collection, a portion remains attracted to us by the resonance it develops with our individual awareness. Thus, it becomes part of our collection and can then be experienced in whatever way.

A simple example is the memory of something that just happened, such as reading these words. Reading these words is a denser reality than the memory of reading these words. This demonstrates that a portion of the experience pattern was captured, the pattern in a sparser form, memory.

To experience reading these words, it is necessary to have resonance with them. That is, there must be harmony between your intent and ability to read the words, and the availability of the words to be read.

All of our experience comes to us as frequency waves. Reading these words comes to you by the light waves between the words and the back of your eyeballs. The basic harmonious relationship between frequency waves is resonance, being on the same wave length, flowing to and through each other, doubling themselves as a team. This is two-way behavior. Experience doesn't just happen to us. We fully cooperate by paying attention to it, which is the only way we have for getting any experience at all.

Therefore, one's response to an opportunity for change must have been created by one's personal resonance with another source of the same wave pattern. Traditionally, that's Mom and Dad, but these days the sources can be many. Simply put, if these wave patterns are available, then they may be resonated with, or picked up or learned.

Whichever kind of patterns is available to a given individual determines the limits of what may be picked up. If one picks up patterns in an environment that emphasize fear, then one is able to resonate with fear. Has one picked up any contenders? No? Then, one's typical response will be fear, the response that is available. This of course is simplified.

We all have a collection of "carrier wavebands," basic modes of functioning in life, enough to see us through our lifetime, although if we stay on the carrier bands, our lives will be monotonous.

These give us a default mode for most of the basic demands of social and physical life. Until we grow out of such default modes, we are essentially trapped in them, repeating the same things over and over. However, these are the modes that "nature" provides us with, each an individualized package deal.

There is nothing stopping us from growing out of these carrier bands. We can choose to sustain the effort needed. Nothing in "nature" can stop us. Except typical response patterns.

When a typical response pattern does pass through one's awareness, such as fear of change, one is helpless to do anything but experience it. Until one chooses to grow out of it.

The process of growing out of typical response patterns is simple to understand when one visualizes the carrier wavebands. They are regular waves going around in a circle.

The pattern of growth is represented by a waveband that creeps up and out of the carrier band, changing its frequency as it goes by resonating with sources that lead to higher upswings and lower downswings.

Everything that can be experienced is traveling frequency wavebands. Frequency wavebands change through resonance with other sources. By managing one's attention along with managing one's goals, one can be deliberate about paying attention to sources that build the frequency wave more than it would naturally build in the carrier wave, and to sources that sustain or diminish it on the downswing.

Do You Feel Vibes from Others? The Rules of Resonance

The resonance or vibes we feel from other people can be described in a clear way.

Resonance comes from radiation between two frequency wave fields.

Simply put, radiation is frequency waves moving away from their source and stimulating resonance in another similar field.

The usual demonstration of resonance is done with two identical tuning forks. One is struck and sings. It is brought close to the other, and it starts the other tuning fork singing, or radiating.

A field is a bunch of frequency waves traveling in a pattern that gives them a shape.

Everything we experience exists as a frequency wave field. Here, we're talking about the radiation from another person and how we can feel radiation from another person's field.

A morphic field is the same thing, a frequency wave field, except it has pronounced self-awareness. It's an actual living entity, and has a living counterpart in Beta reality.

By studying the patterns of a morphic field, we can learn what it is aware of, and we can identify its purpose.

Every experience involves resonance with a pattern, a morphic field. By seeing experience this way, we can be aware of the rules of resonance and solve many of our puzzles about experience.

Every morphic field has its own frequencies. While we cannot change the frequencies of a morphic field, we can change the frequency our attention is tuned to. We have four wavebands, according to brainwave research.

We are typically oriented to one of our wavebands more than the others. Resonance is what tells us whether a person is resonating from mind or body senses (or perhaps even from Alpha or dream reality).

For resonance to occur between two human morphic fields, three rules apply. These apply to resonance between any two morphic fields.

Resonant Rule

Both entities must be capable of resonating on the same frequencies.

As mentioned, the key here is tuning our attention to the morphic field's. We have the following frequency bands to choose from: Beta, Alpha, Theta and Delta.

In the Beta range of 14 to 30 Hz, we can resonate with morphic fields of our physical reality, mind and body.

In the Alpha range of 8 to 13 Hz, we can resonate with morphic fields of our daydream reality—thoughts, imaginings, memories.

In the Theta range of 4 to 7 Hz, we can resonate with morphic fields of our dream reality, common dreams.

In the Delta range of 0.5 to 3 Hz, we can resonate with morphic fields in all three ranges at the same time.

In addition, we can be in tune with intuition itself, which can resonate with any frequency.

Power Rule

The power of one's resonance must be strong enough to stimulate resonance in the other.

This power sets the strength of the vibes we feel and put out.

Power here refers to the amplitude of resonance of a morphic field of frequency waves.

If we radiate toward someone on a common frequency, we can stimulate resonance in them, overpower their state of not resonating, because we have greater amplitude on the same frequency.

Consistency Rule

One's strong resonance must be directed continuously until resonance in the other has been stimulated (homeostasis overcome).

This involves persistent focus or tuning. It applies to everyday realities as well as to realities in other dimensions.

When we pick up on another person's radiation, we can identify whether it is from their mind or their body. Once we learn to recognize this, and it happens routinely but we don't usually pay direct attention to it, we can choose whether to resonate on that same frequency or refuse, and whether to initiate resonance on a different frequency and try to get them to resonate accordingly.

This can eliminate lots of the hassles of interpersonal relations, and replace them with harmony.

Create Reality with Morphic Robots

The decades of the New Age movement have aroused considerable interest in a mystery—that we create our own reality.

A lot has been written, a lot discussed, about exactly how we do this. Some people have one or more pieces of the puzzle, enough to get results sometimes for some people but not all of the time for all of the people.

The key to our interest in this process, of course, is the thought, "If I create my own reality, then I want it to be different." Most of us are looking for ways to improve the reality we experience.

Hordes of us are working jobs we do not enjoy, working to fulfill someone else's purpose.

Most of us have some relationships filled with frictions that make reality miserable.

The truth we accept is a bothersome problem for many of us—is belief enough? Is science too much?

If we do create our own reality, we can expect there to be a process involved. We should be able to prove it by, first, understanding the process, and then by witnessing it in operation all around us.

Understanding the process opens the door for taking direct action and changing the results, the reality that we experience.

To make this work for us, we first need to orient ourselves to an updated understanding of reality.

Reality is what we experience. The only access we have to reality is by experiencing it in our awareness. The only reality we are aware of is the reality inside, in our awareness.

This is easy enough to observe in ourselves as the way it is (although our Beta minds fight the idea).

Creating reality, then, is creating a flow of experience.

We can reduce everything about reality to a flow of experience, flowing through our awareness. That's the bottom line of reality.

What actually are flowing are frequency wave interference fields, called morphic fields.

The patterns in these fields produce experience.

When we are deliberately creating, changing or destroying an experience pattern, we call it a morphic robot. It's just a way of saying that we've had our hands on this pattern.

Creating a morphic robot is a six-step process. These steps are inspiration, incubation, adoption, construction, vivification, manifestation.

Inspiration gives us contact with the possibilities we might experience. There is a skill for tuning our attention in to inspiration.

Tuning our attention to Alpha gives us access to the experience patterns we already have, those we have accumulated since we were little dots of awareness.

Tuning our attention to Beta gives us access to the way our experience patterns look in physical reality. Again, these are the same patterns that we already have.

To experience new possibilities, new experience patterns, we need to focus our attention somewhere else, outside of our own Alpha and Beta storehouse.

The approach to gathering new experience patterns comes from the contact of our awareness itself with the outside universe. We can tune in to this by withdrawing our attention from Alpha and Beta, and focusing it on intuition. That way, we can pay attention to the patterns coming in from outside of ourselves, and identify the new possibilities that fit our goal by their resonance.

Incubation means we examine the possibility. We keep it alive while we consider it for our purpose.

This work is done partly in Alpha and partly in Beta.

In Alpha, where we deal with the patterns themselves, we can play around with patterns, try fitting them together into new combinations, and just see what can be done with them.

In Beta, we do logical work with the patterns, making them add up to a process that makes logical sense. And, we assess our resources and opportunities for manifesting the patterns.

Adoption is our decision to commit to the possibility we have developed. We have now become the parent of a robot.

Construction is the design and testing of a process for our robot. Here, we create a step-by-step series of experience patterns that result in our goal, or create the possibility.

We can devote more or less care to construction. The more care we put into it, the more precise our resulting experience will be. Construction is work, and many people slack off at this step. Too bad.

Vivification is giving life to the possibility, infusing it with awareness so that it has an independent existence as a living entity.

A new robot pattern in Alpha is just a pattern. It has no life. Life is awareness.

Awareness is increased in the pattern through resonance, making the patterns produce higher amplitudes when they pass through our window of NOW.

We can do two things to increase the resonance of a new robot. We can hold it in our window of NOW and resonate with it by paying attention to it. The more we do this, the more the amplitude or resonance of the pattern will build up, according to the rules of resonance.

When we have developed control over emotion, we can add emotion to the process of increasing resonance, by feeling strong emotion at the same time we hold the pattern in our window of NOW.

Manifestation is both witnessing and assisting the robot to become a reality in our experience. This is where we shuffle our feet, actually give aid to the robot in its first manifestations in Beta, and help it to step through its process.

We are on the alert for signs that the robot is beginning to manifest in Beta. We interpret our experiences in terms of their patterns. When we see our robot's pattern in a Beta experience, we help that experience to manifest, by hand.

Two steps are post-creation. Maintenance involves updating the robot.

Interruption involves uncreating a robot when we no longer want it.

A morphic robot may be less than human, but it does have awareness of its existence and purpose, and it is capable of iterating its process. It can perform without the support of our attention.

A morphic robot, then, can operate more or less invisibly, independent of our direction. We can confirm that it is operating by watching the signs of manifestation.

Depending on how complicated our morphic robot is, we can observe its manifestation by watching the changes that occur in our reality that bring us steps closer to experiencing the robot's pattern.

The thing that separates the signs of manifestation from what would have happened anyway is the surprising way that events and circumstances bring the necessary opportunities to us. We call this synchronicity, or surprising coincidence.

This is actually the design work of the robot, arranging Beta events and circumstances toward its manifestation.

All of our experience occurs the same way, from a constant flow of experience patterns developed over time. We're isolating the robots because we purposefully created their patterns.

Changing our reality is a two-edged sword because change involves both gaining something new and releasing something old. Change replaces something, and that some thing needs to be sacrificed. These sacrifices, which can feel like "little suicides" if we think they are part of ourselves, involve unwanted morphic robots.

As we learn to create new robots, we must also learn how to interrupt our resonance with old ones which will be replaced. This also applies to each individual pattern in the robot, when we are just changing it.

Robots should be treated with respect as living entities. They are. Depending on their complexity, they can be considered quasi-humans, pets or living machines. They are in fact our slaves, and we need to be benevolent slave masters with them.

Some Key Morphic Robots

Our experience is determined by the morphic robots that resonate strongly enough to attract our attention. Most of these robots have been created unwittingly.

One of our great powers is the ability to create morphic robots (the morphic fields we are purposely changing) that provide us with new experience. We do it whether we know it or not.

When we know this, we can create our own morphic robots on purpose and literally manage our future experience.

And we can get rid of or modify those old robots that are just no longer wanted, robots that have finished serving their purpose in our life.

We'll consider a few examples of robots that play key parts in our experience: habit, fear and guilt.

Habit

Habits are easy-to-see examples of morphic robots. Creating a habit takes the same six steps as creating a morphic robot, and you can see this by tracing one of your habits back through this process to what inspired it in the first place.

A habit has its own awareness. It knows just when to kick in and produce its pattern in experience. It operates independently.

Habit is a great simplifier for repetitive experiences that we don't want to recreate from scratch every time. Life would be a hopeless mess without habits.

And life can be a hopeless mess with habits, depending on what they are. Thoughtfully recreating one's habits so that they produce harmonious experience is a reward of building morphic robots.

Fear

Fear is a primitive morphic robot, dating back to mankind's earliest experiences when we were hunted animals. It is powerful because it is directly resonant with emotion. Usually, we call it an emotion because of this relationship.

Emotion itself is pure resonant power of resonance in a pattern. What we call specific emotions, such as fear, are patterns with an identity in experience.

An emotional pattern may be strong, but it because it is primitive, it can be interrupted by a morphic robot designed in a more complex or more highly developed system.

Guilt

Guilt is another emotional robot, and in all likelihood was first created by parents as a tool to control their children.

Guilt always relates to a conflict in truth. It resonates with the truths of blind faith and speculation. It never resonates with the truths of reason or science because these do not resonate with emotion, and they process conflicting truths toward resolution.

The experience of guilt can be interrupted by robots created with a rational design.

Where Does a Habit Get Its Power?

Our habits carry us through our days, automating many of our routine activities. We don't have to think; we just act. What is it that gives a habit the power to act without requiring us to think about it?

A habit is an example of a morphic robot at work. As you've read in my writings (I hope), a morphic robot is a pattern with a purpose, and it has consciousness of its own. It gets this consciousness from contact (resonance) with our own awareness, during the process of its creation.

Before resonance can occur between two patterns, three requisites must be met. The two patterns must be capable of resonance (in harmony with each other); one must be strong enough (have high amplitude) to overcome the stable, non-resonating state of the other; and the strong one must be persistent enough to develop the resonance.

The power of a habit comes from persistence. It is the nature of a habit to persist. Once resonance is established between two patterns (the pattern we have created in our own consciousness, and the pattern that is the morphic robot), the habit or robot will literally have a life of its own.

Thoughts on Purpose

Once we understand consciousness, we understand everything big and small. We understand ourselves, our realities, and our universe. Is there a purpose to it all? Can we now see the purpose in our own lives?

The apparent purpose of our existence is experience. The universe as an entity has no purpose. It has only homogenized possibility.

Each of us is the universe, in a holographic sense. We are each strapped into an attention system that enables us to experience. Experience is necessarily individual. Each individual's experience is different. Each of us is a fresh opportunity for the universe to add to its experience. Thus, each fresh experience of ours is something new for the universe.

Is there purpose in life? It is experience, the very ability to experience. Does it make much difference what we experience? The important realization is that there is nothing and no one out there judging us or our experience. We are the universe, and we are the only judge.

So how do we judge our own experience? Perhaps we need to be attentive to opportunities for new experience, rather than bore the universe with the same old same old.

When someone is experiencing something different from us, that is cause for celebration, for the universe is receiving variety. The wisdom in the expression, "Be Yourself," stems from the uniqueness of each individual and the fresh experience each individual can contribute to the universe.

Well, that's fine for them, but what about ourselves? Each of us has a purpose in a lifetime, a line of experience to pursue, built into our default experience patterns. We can identify our purpose by looking at the ways we are limited or restricted. We can look at our talents, interests, abilities, aptitudes, handicaps, circumstances and opportunities.

All of these prevent us from choosing most of the possible purposes in life, leaving open only certain possibilities. Each of us is pointed in a particular direction, each different from the other. Each of us experiences a unique life that is a gift from and to a universe that would have no experience at all but for limited consciousness systems, including those like us.

Each of us has the opportunity to broaden this experience to include additional dimensions of reality, to discover more about ourselves, our multi-dimensional environment, and our universe. We can even go back home to the universal entity, satisfy ourselves that we belong to it and that it needs us, and return to life wiser and more compassionate.

Who Are You?

Who are you?

How are you going to answer?

Are you going to tell me what you do for a living? Is that who you are? Then, who will you be when you retire? Who are you?

Are you going to tell me about your family tree? Is that who you are, a descendant? I mean, who are YOU?

Are you going to tell me about what you own? Is your stuff who you are? So who will you be after you go bankrupt? Who are you??

Are you going to tell me what your body looks like? So, as your body goes, you go, too? Is that who you are?

Are you going to tell me your interests? Is that who you are? Well, who were you before you had these interests? And who will you be after you lose interest in these? Who are you?

Are you going to tell me about your beliefs? Is that how you define yourself? Who were you before you had these beliefs? And who will you be after your beliefs change? Who are you?

Are you going to tell me about your conquests? Your victories? Or your failures? No, I mean, in between these things, who are you?

Are you going to tell me about your skills and talents? Is that who you are? In that case, who are you when you're doing something else? Who are you?

Are you going to tell me about your appetites, your desires, your cravings? Really? That's who you are? Come on, who are you?

Are you going to tell me about your hobbies, your favorite music, soaps, movie stars and writers? You mean, what you like is who you are? Get out of here, who are you really?

Are you going to tell me where you live? What kind of car you drive? Where you buy your clothes? You mean, these are who you are?

Are you going to tell me about your past, your memories, and your experiences? What about now? Who are you now?

Are you going to tell me how much money you have? Do you mean that who you are varies according to your bank balance? Really, who are you?

Are you going to tell me about the famous people you know, the status person you're married to, who your famous company is, or some other reputation that you trade on?

No, I'm asking, who are YOU?

Well? Cat got your tongue? What, no answer for me? Want a clue?

Do you know the difference between who you are and what you experience?

www.ingramcontent.com/pod-product-compliance
Lightning Source LLC
LaVergne TN
LVHW041621070426
835507LV00008B/369